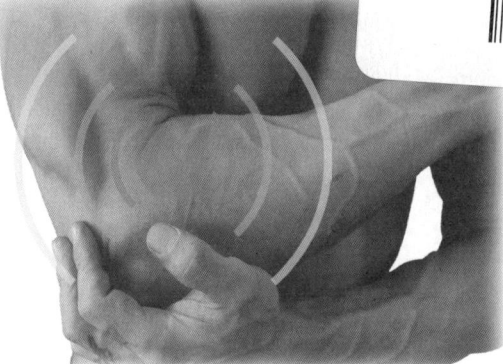

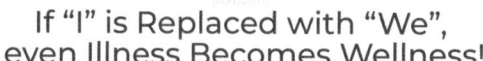

If "I" is Replaced with "We", even Illness Becomes Wellness!

Congratulations on taking an active role in your health through education and increasing your knowledge base. This research based text, along with recommendations from your health care professionals are a great place to facilitate this process; especially with their advice and recommendations for **your individualized specific needs**. You play a critical role in the patient centered approach to healthcare, your needs and opinion count! As a general rule, we should progress from **least invasive to most invasive processes, with a focus on minimal effective dose.**

What are the proven most effective treatment options with the least effort. **Work smarter, not harder to get better faster and stay stronger longer.**

This book will facilitate your journey by teaching you 3 key steps:

1. **Education** to create a foundation of understanding

2. **Assessment** methods to find the **true cause** of the pain or injury

3. **Actions** to consider for treatment, exercise, follow-up and referrals

Realize you are not alone, and we are here to help promote your optimal recovery and performance.

Dr. Vizniak **prohealthsys.com**

Education

Scientists generally recognize five determinants of health:

Individual behavior - Yours to Control!
- **Diet** (eat whole, unprocessed foods)
- **Physical activity** (just do it!) - According to the world health organization Physical Inactivity is the 4th leading cause of global mortality
- **Sleep** (this is where you recover)
- Poor 'foods,' alcohol, cigarette & drugs

Genetics and biology
- **Age** (you can be physiologically younger by the choices you make)
- Gender & Inherited conditions (genetics)

Social determinants
- Availability of resources to meet daily needs (education, jobs, real foods)
- Exposure to crime, violence, and social disorder (eg. trash or discrimination)
- Transportation options & public safety

Environment determinants
- Natural environment (plants, forests, weather, climate, light and pets)
- Built environment (buildings, workstation ergonomics, transportation)
- Toxic substances, physical hazards and barriers (esp. for disabled individuals)

Health services determinants
- Both **access and quality are key**
- Lack of **good quality** availability
- Limited language access, high cost

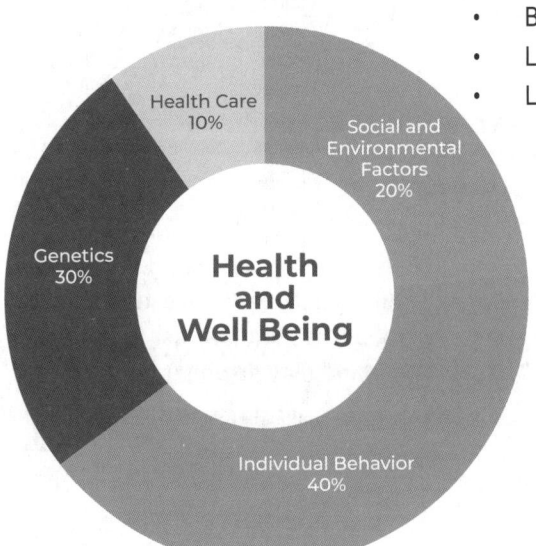

You can control your behavior, healthcare and many social/environmental factors and can influence your genetic expression

Factors that IMPROVE healing

1. **Laughter, positive mood & good sleep**
2. **Love, community & social support**
3. **Adequate nutrition (food is medicine)** - whole unprocessed foods
4. **Younger physiologic age** (life choices)
5. **Good blood supply** (nutrient/waste exchange)
6. **Aerobic fitness, activity & movement**
7. **Soft tissue/joint mobilization & massage**
8. **Electrotherapeutics** (microcurrent, laser, ultrasound) & **Acupuncture**
9. **Surgical interventions** (last resort)
10. **Lower toxic load** (environmental & social)
11. **Confidence in future wellness & health care provider's ability** (positive expectations)

Things You Can Control

Your Gratitude

Your Physique

Your Habits

Your Network

Your Work Rate

Your Attitude

Your attitude determines your altitude.

12 SCIENTIFIC WAYS TO IMPROVE HAPPINESS

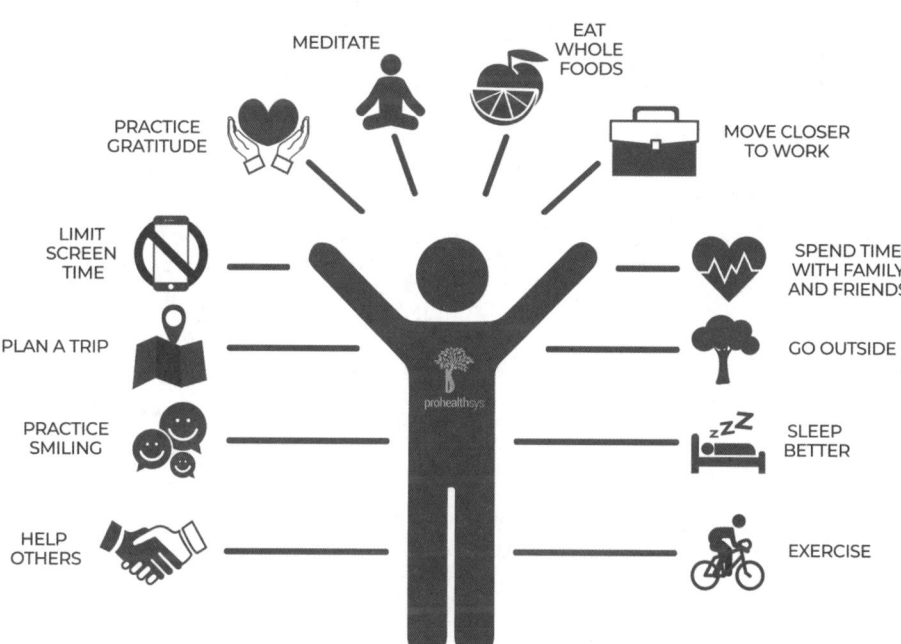

PRACTICE GRATITUDE

MEDITATE

EAT WHOLE FOODS

MOVE CLOSER TO WORK

LIMIT SCREEN TIME

SPEND TIME WITH FAMILY AND FRIENDS

PLAN A TRIP

GO OUTSIDE

PRACTICE SMILING

SLEEP BETTER

HELP OTHERS

EXERCISE

prohealthsys

Education

The human body is designed to move.

For 1,000's of years, that's exactly what we did. With urbanization & technological advances (cars, TV, computers, tractors) physical activity levels have been steadily dropping. As technology does more of the heavy lifting, people become increasingly sedentary. The impact our sedentary lifestyles (in office, school or home) may be one of the most unanticipated health threats of our modern time (sitting disease). The graph on the right shows the average ADLs for most urban dwellers in north America (source: BLS & NIH)

Sitting disease - *metabolic syndrome & ill-effects of an overly sedentary lifestyle*

Did you know? Physical Inactivity is the 4th leading cause of mortality in North America...

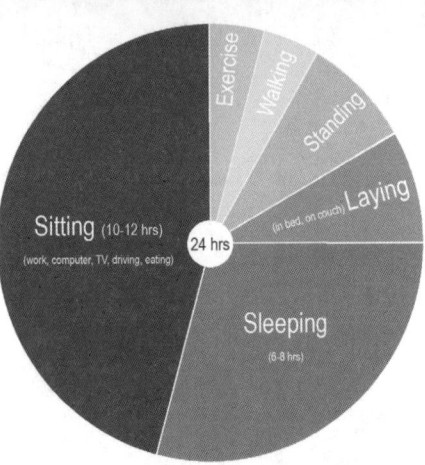

- **Prolonged sedentary time is independently associated with negative health outcomes regardless of physical activity!** - even if you engage in the doctor-recommended 150 minutes of moderate to vigorous activity per week, you are still subject to the negative impact of too much sitting.

- **Low intensity, 'non-exercise' activities like standing and walking are much more important than most realize.** Low level activities play a crucial metabolic role and account for more of our daily energy expenditure than moderate-to-high intensity activities if they are done over a long enough period of time

With **simple lifestyle changes** we can make big changes and reduce the risks. Research shows that if we choose to stand up, move more and sit less, we can experience a many benefits to our health, minds and bodies. On the most basic level, **alternate sitting and standing every 30 minutes for optimal health**.

Benefits if we sit less, stand up and move more.

1. **Bone/joint health** - require regular movement to maintain strength – low-level activity helps improve your bone health to reduce the risk of osteoporosis (rates are on the rise)

2. **Muscles** - position changes enlist large muscle groups. Unused, weak muscles leave joints unstable and prone to injury and chronic pain. Sitting makes hips tight, which can affect posture, balance & ROM. Gluteal muscles

weaken from lack of use ('dormant butt syndrome' or 'gluteal amnesia') becoming soft and undefined from lack of use.

3. **Reduced cancer risk** - Studies have linked prolonged sitting to a greater risk for colon, breast and endometrial cancers; regular movement increase antioxidant levels. Those who are physically active have a 40% decrease in cancer mortality.

4. **Brain power** - standing delivers more oxygen and nutrients to the brain through improved blood flow. Physical activity enhances neurogenesis in regions of the brain associated with critical thinking. Research shows in the classroom how that movement strengthens learning and improves memory and retrieval

5. **Improved Mood** - Sitting for 6+ hours during the workday puts you at a higher risk for anxiety and depression. In several studies, **100% of workers and students** reported positive effects on mood states and productivity after reducing sitting time.

6. There are many, many more...

- Smith L, Hamer M, Ucci M, et al. Weekday and weekend patterns of objectively measured sitting, standing, and stepping in a sample of office-based workers: the active buildings study. BMC Public Health. 2015;15:9.
- Aggio D, Wallace K, Boreham N, Shankar A, Steptoe A, Hamer M. Objectively Measured Daily Physical Activity and Postural Changes as Related to Positive and Negative Affect Using Ambulatory Monitoring Assessments. Psychosomatic Medicine. 2017;79(7):792-797. doi:10.1097/PSY.0000000000000485.
- The pandemic of physical inactivity: global action for public health. Kohl HW 3rd, Craig CL, Lambert EV, Inoue S, Alkandari JR, Leetongin G, Kahlmeier S, Lancet Physical Activity Series Working Group. Lancet. 2012 Jul 21; 380(9838):294-305.

Disease is stagnation, motion is the potion

The Power of DIET and EXERCISE

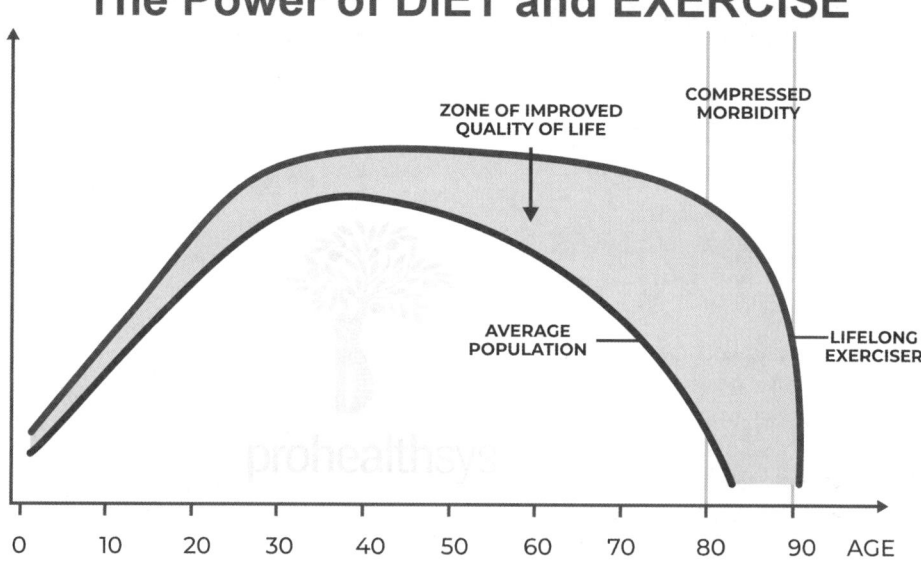

ZONE OF IMPROVED
QUALITY OF LIFE

COMPRESSED
MORBIDITY

AVERAGE
POPULATION

LIFELONG
EXERCISER

0 10 20 30 40 50 60 70 80 90 AGE

Standing meetings
Stand or walk
during meetings to
improve engagement

Work standing,
burns 40% more
calories than sitting

Talk in person
Talk to co-
workers rather
then text or email

Walking break,
whenever possible
eat lunch out of office

WAYS TO
INCREASE
MOVEMENT
AT WORK

Move
Squat at your desk
Use your big muscles
to improve health

Water
Stay hydrated,
walk to the bathroom

Walk around
when talking on
the phone

Stretch & Move
every 45 min
at your desk

Sleep is when you recover physically and mentally. Healthy sleep habits can make a huge difference in your quality of life. Sleep benefits include:

1. Improved mood and function
2. Better maintenance of body weight (yes you can burn fat in your sleep)
3. Improved immune function
4. Look more attractive
5. Lower risk of injury

Practice a relaxing bedtime ritual away from bright lights. A relaxing routine helps separate your sleep time from activities that can cause excitement, stress or anxiety which can make it more difficult to fall asleep. Spend the last hour before bed doing a calming activity such as reading. **Avoid electronics before bed or in the middle of the night.**

"Remove electrons from your room"

Exercise daily. Vigorous exercise is best, but even light exercise is better than no activity. Exercise at any time of day, but not at the expense of your sleep.

Bedroom Setup

- Temperature cool ~18°C (60°F)

- **Quiet and dark** (consider using blackout curtains, eye shades, ear plugs, "white noise" machines, fans etc.)

- Comfortable mattress and pillows (mattress life expectancy ~10 years)

- **No work materials, computers, phones and TVs** in sleeping environment. Use your bed only for sleep and sex to strengthen the association between bed and sleep.

See the Morning Light. Your body's internal clock is sensitive to light and darkness, so getting a dose of the sun first thing in the morning will help you wake up. **Avoid bright light in the evening, especially blue light.** This will keep your circadian rhythms in check.

It's not just what you eat—it's when you eat. While you know that it's not a good idea to go to bed on an empty stomach, being stuffed is just as bad. **Avoid alcohol, cigarettes, and heavy meals in the evening**. Avoid eating large meals for two to three hours before bedtime. Try a light snack 45 minutes before bed if you're still hungry.

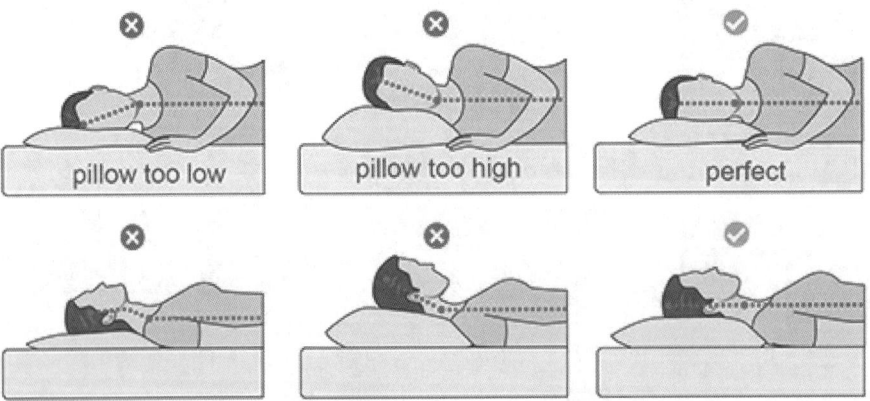

| pillow too low | pillow too high | perfect |

~30% of our life is spent sleeping. It is crucial to evaluate sleep systems, habits & positions

13 WAYS TO IMPROVE YOUR SLEEP

GET 15-30 MINUTES OF SUNLIGHT EACH MORNING

USE YOUR BEDROOM ONLY FOR SLEEP AND SEX

AVOID ALCOHOL BEFORE BED

WAKE UP AND GO TO BED AT THE SAME TIME. SLEEP 7-8 HOURS

DO RELAXING ACTIVITIES BEFORE BED

DO NOT WATCH TV OR WORK ON YOUR COMPUTER AND DO NOT USE GADGETS BEFORE BEDTIME

TAKE A WARM BATH OR SHOWER BEFORE BEDTIME

DRINKING A WARM CUP OF TEA OR GLASS OF MILK

READ A BOOK OR LISTEN TO A RELAXING MUSIC

AVOID OVEREATING AT DINNER AND AVOID CONSUMING CAFFEINE IN THE LATE AFTERNOON

AVOID LIGHTS WHEN TRYING TO SLEEP

STOP EXERCISING FOUR HOURS BEFORE BEDTIME

COMFORTABLE TEMPERATURE IN THE BEDROOM

prohealthsys

1. **Focus on GOALS**

2. **Bringing awareness** into the body. Many people with pain disconnect from their body and injured regions. We need to help re-establish the mind-body connection and begin to accept it even with pain. Deep relaxed breathing with intentional focus can facilitate this process.

3. **Differentiate & recognize** pain vs sensation. In chronic pain the boundaries between pain and sensation can be blurred. Recognize sensations for what they are and not confuse them with pain.

4. **Identifying contributing factors** (activities/behaviors) in activities of daily living that make pain worse. Encourage *reduction, modification* or *elimination* of these factors. Habits may be among the biggest contributors to healing (activity, diet & psychosocial).

5. **Discover** positions that are pain free (in supine, kneeling, seating and standing positions). These positions will be a starting point for movement and you can always return back to them and rest there without pain. Then look for motions that do NOT cause pain. Explore **with movement first from the spine and extend out into the limbs**. It's vital to find movements without or very little pain - start from this safe place.

6. **Recognize & respect** movements that cause pain. At the start, avoid movement that causes pain to develop a safe zone to move without pain. As movement progresses it might be possible to *explore* some of those movements if the progression is warranted and serves to strengthen and stabilize the body. **Pain should always be respected but challenged.**

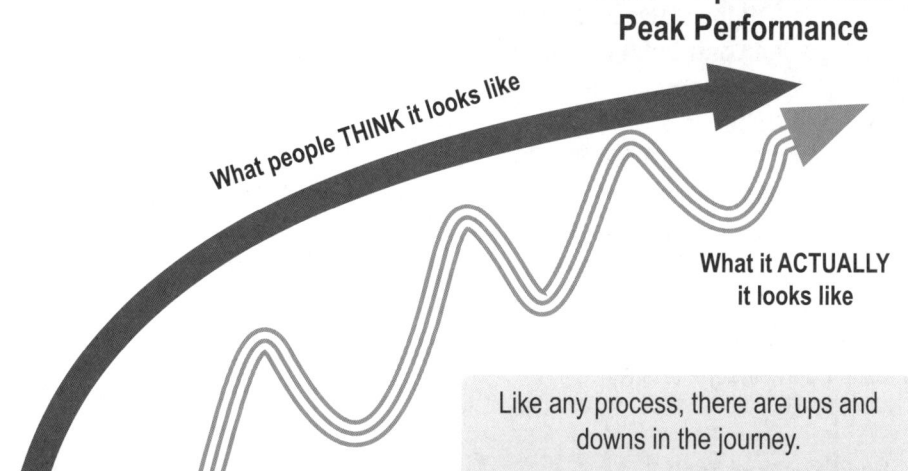

Goal = Optimal Health Peak Performance

What people THINK it looks like

What it ACTUALLY it looks like

Like any process, there are ups and downs in the journey.

Celebrate the small victories!

FEAR AVOIDANCE MODEL

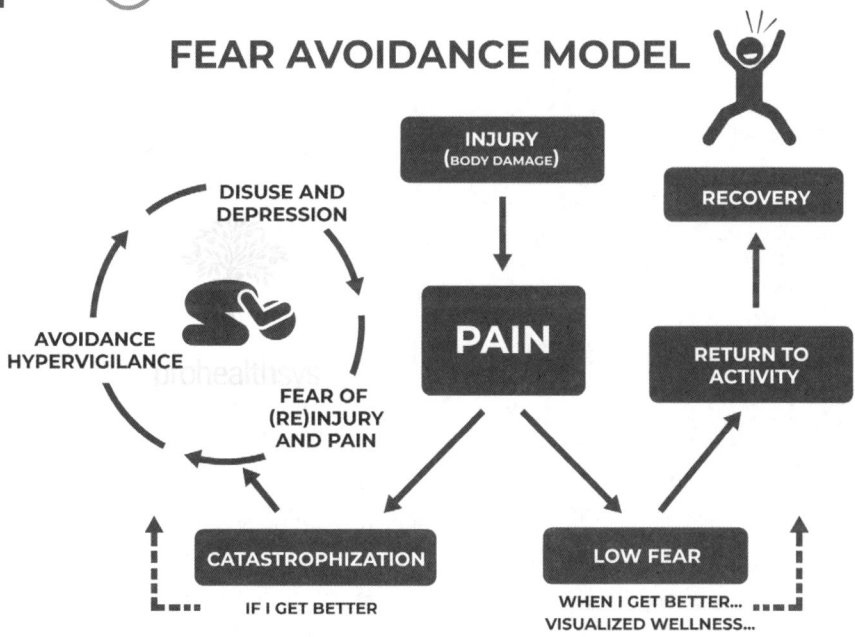

INJURY
(BODY DAMAGE)

DISUSE AND DEPRESSION

RECOVERY

AVOIDANCE HYPERVIGILANCE

PAIN

RETURN TO ACTIVITY

FEAR OF (RE)INJURY AND PAIN

CATASTROPHIZATION

IF I GET BETTER

LOW FEAR

WHEN I GET BETTER... VISUALIZED WELLNESS...

Catastrophization, avoidance & fear of future injury creates a cycle for the development of chronic pain. Research & personal experience show that the best chance for recovery is a return to normal activities of daily living (ADL). **It is important to have this conversation with people for their own understanding & healing. - Where are you in this cycle?**

--- Focus on goals, not injuries ---

prohealthsys

The most important factor in optimal health is to find the true cause(s) of pathology and contributing factors. This starts with an investigative process of **history, inspection and palpation** (hands on assessment); followed by **motion evaluation**, and if indicated **neurovascular** and **special tests** (orthopedics, xray, MRI). **The most important part of any evaluation is the history**. Below are some detailed question that must be answered:

1. What are your goals? _____

_____

_____

_____

2. Location, where is the issue exactly? _____

_____

_____

_____

_____

3. When & how did it start? _____

_____

_____

_____

4. How severe is it or does it affect any of your daily activities? _____

_____

_____

_____

5. What makes it worse? _____

_____

_____

_____

6. What makes it better? _____

_____

_____

_____

7. Prior treatments tried, and what has worked or not worked? (medication, rest, heat, exercise) _____

_____

_____

_____

_____

Helping evaluate these parameters can **give a good baseline** of function and create a list of **outcome markers** we can use to evaluate progression and focus the physical exam

Inspection will usually include a **posture and gait evaluation**, followed by a motion and hands on assessment.

On the next page is a **summary table** that can be used to help identify the specific tissue or structures that could be causing some of the issues.

Your healthcare team are experts in this investigative process, which allows them to give you the best possible recommendations and care.

prohealthsys

Education

Tissue Type	AROM	PROM	RROM	Comments
Muscle Injury (strain or tendinopathy)	↓ AROM (painful)	WNL (pain at end ROM)	Pain	• Dull ache - sharp pain when challenged • **Pain with palpation, stretching or contraction of damaged muscle** (possible weakness)
Ligament Injury (sprain)	↓ AROM (painful)	↓ PROM (painful)	WNL (painless)	• Injured at full end ROM with tearing • **Pain with palpation or stretching** of ligament (passive over pressure) • **Instability** due to full ligament rupture may show an empty end feel, ↑ PROM or repeatable 'clunk' with motion
Joint Injury (arthropathy)	↓ AROM (painful)	↓ PROM (painful)	WNL (painless)	• Mild loss of ROM or pain • **Crepitus with scour test** • AROM may show repeatable 'snapping' & 'popping' ; Pain changes with weather
Joint Dysfunction (subluxation)	WNL or limited segmental ROM	Limited in specific ROM	WNL or weak	• Pain or point tenderness • Asymmetry/misalignment • **PROM abnormality or restriction** - joint "feels stuck"
Bone Injury (fracture)	↓ AROM (painful)	↓ PROM (painful)	↓ RROM (painful)	• Hx of trauma - **perform fracture screen** • Pin point tenderness, dull ache but very sharp when challenged
Nerve Injury	↓ or WNL	WNL	Weak	• **Numbness, tingling or muscle weakness** & shooting electrical pain with stretch or compression of nerve
Visceral Injury (organs)	• Writhing or **cramping pain** secondary to internal organ capsule distension or vascular compromise, deep achy, often **poorly localized** & may be immobilizing in more severe cases (eg. intestinal cramps, PMS, appendicitis) - pain is often **NOT relieved by change in body position**			

AROM = active range of motion, PROM = passive ROM, RROM = resisted ROM (muscle testiong), ↑ = increase, ↓ = decrease, WNL = within normal limits, Hx = history, **World Health Organization 'Subluxation' definition** - "A lesion or dysfunction in a joint or motion segment in which alignment, movement integrity and/or physiological function are altered, although contact between joint surfaces remains intact. It is essentially a functional entity, which may influence biomechanical and neural integrity."

The 6 best doctors

HEALTHY EATING

SOCIAL TIME

OUTDOOR WALKS

EXERCISE

REST

SUNLIGHT

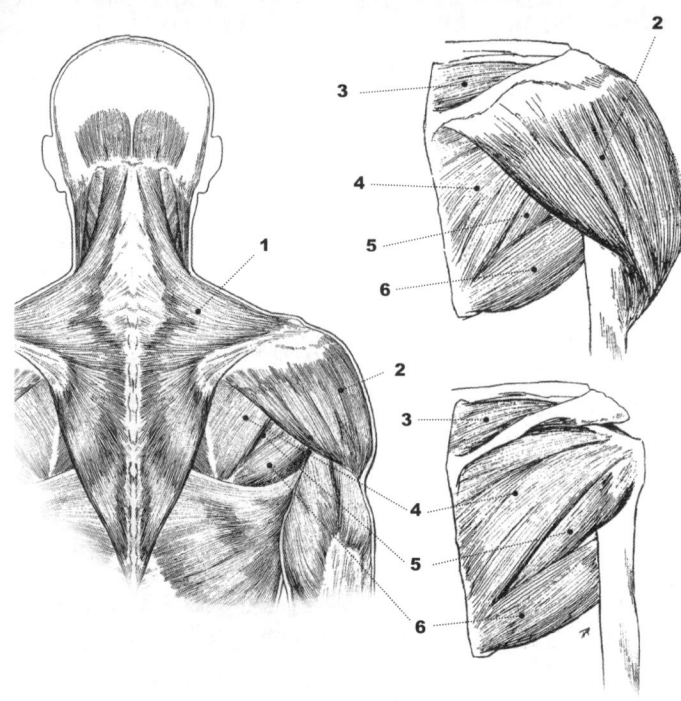

1. Trapezius
2. Deltoid
3. Supraspinatus
4. Infraspinatus
5. Teres minor
6. Teres major
7. Subscapularis
8. Serratus anterior
9. Pectoralis major
10. Latissimus dorsi

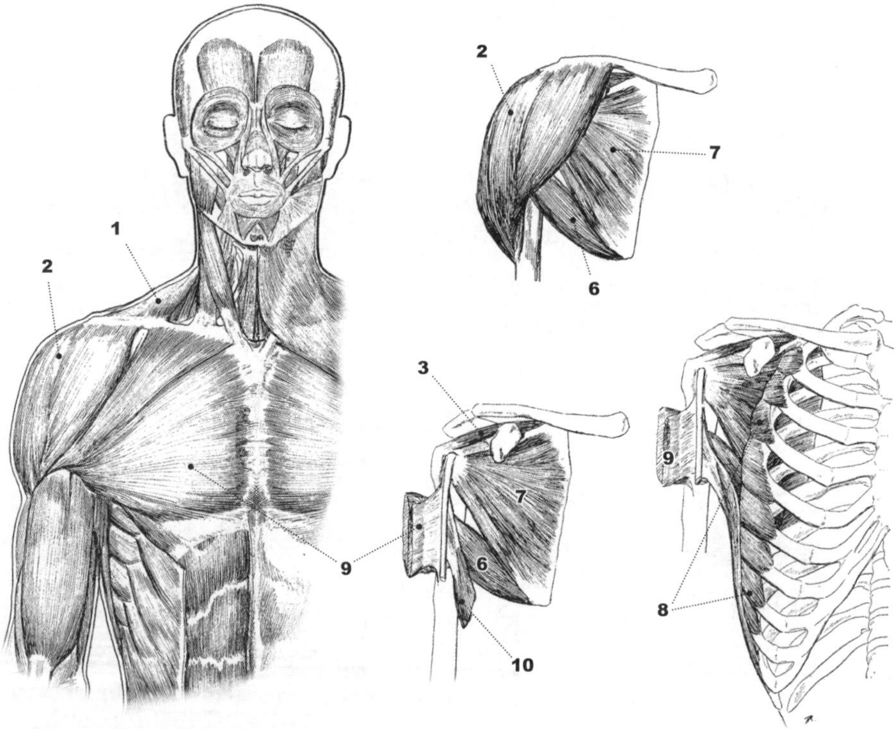

1

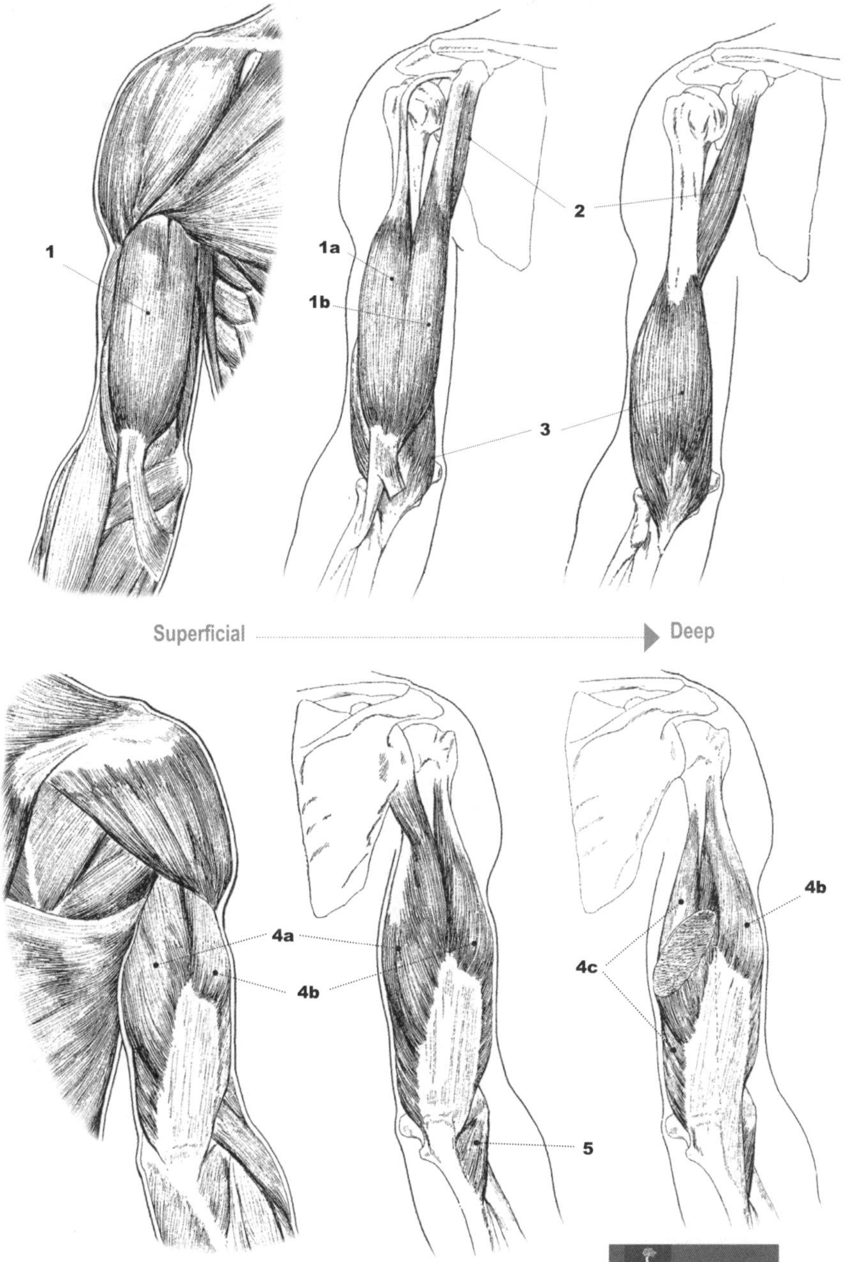

1a
1b

2

3

Superficial ⸻▶ Deep

4a
4b

4b
4c

5

1. Biceps brachii
   a. Long head
   b. Short Head
2. Coracobrachialis
3. Brachialis

4. Triceps brachii
   a. Long head
   b. Lateral head
   c. Deep (medial) head
5. Anconeus

MUSCLE MANUAL

Learn More

Forearm Muscles

prohealthsys

1. Brachioradialis
2. Pronator teres (superficial head)
3. Flexor carpi radialis
4. Palmaris longus
5. Flexor carpi ulnaris
6. Flexor digitorum superficialis
7. Flexor digitorum profundus
8. Flexor pollicis longus
9. Pronator teres (deep head)
10. Supinator
11. Pronator quadratus

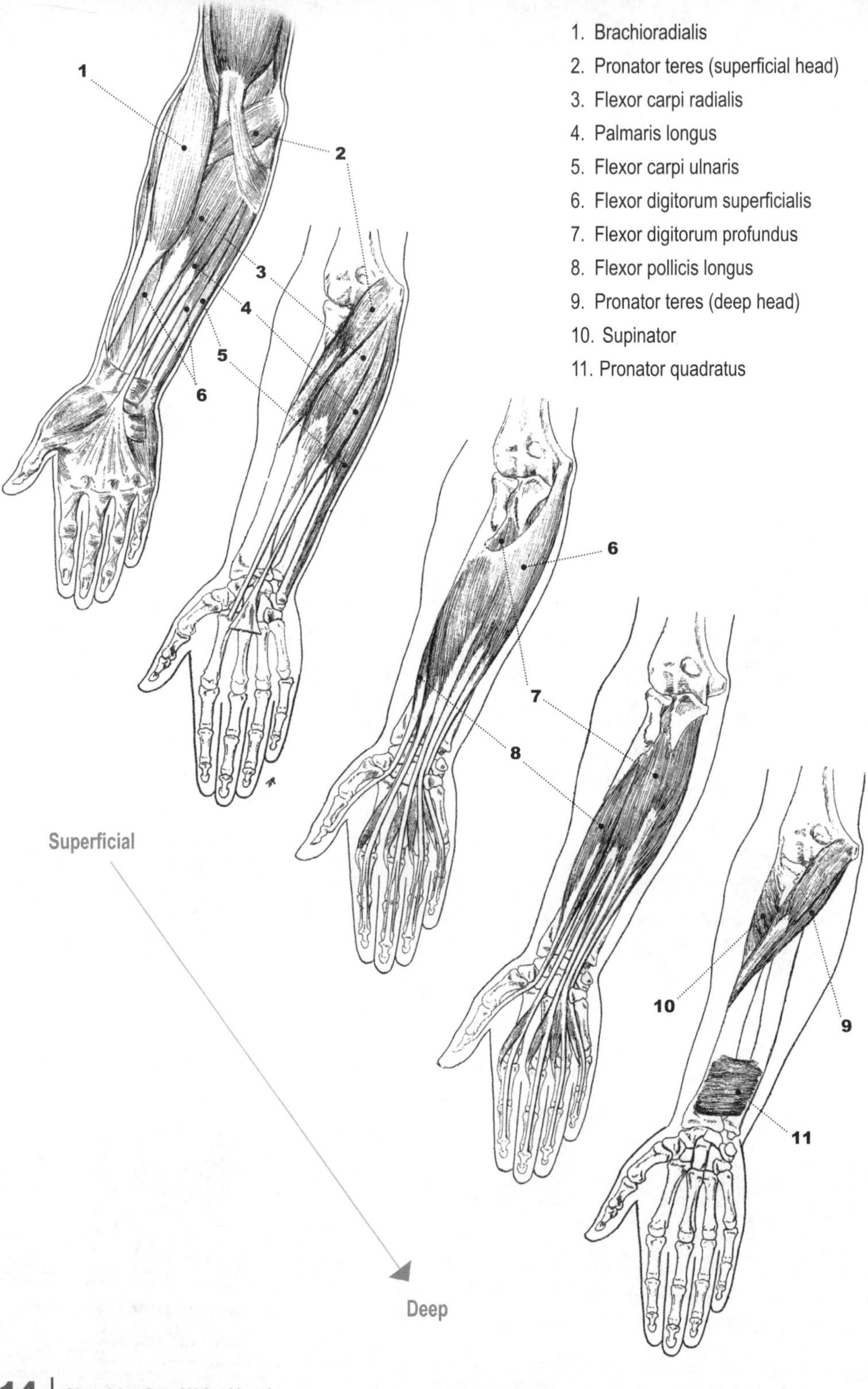

1
2
3
4
5
6
6
7
8
10
9
11
Superficial
Deep

prohealthsys

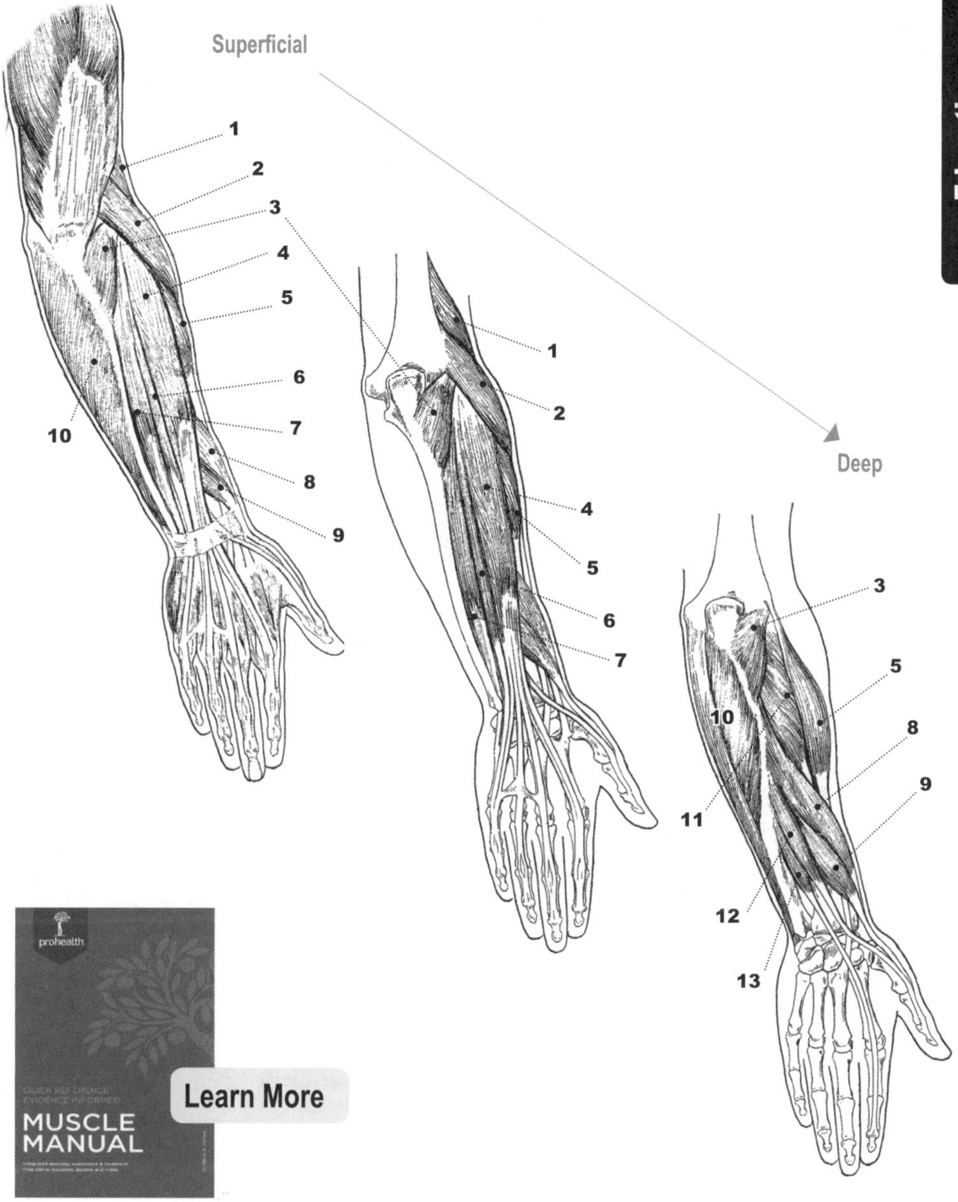

Superficial

1
2
3
4
5
6
7
8
9
10

1
2
4
5
6
7

Deep

3
5
8
9
10
11
12
13

MUSCLE
MANUAL

Learn More

1. Brachioradialis
2. Extensor carpi radialis longus
3. Anconeus
4. Extensor digitorum
5. Extensor carpi radialis brevis
6. Extensor digiti minimi
7. Extensor carpi ulnaris
8. Abductor pollicis longus
9. Extensor pollicis brevis
10. Flexor carpi ulnaris
11. Supinator
12. Extensor pollicis longus
13. Extensor indicis

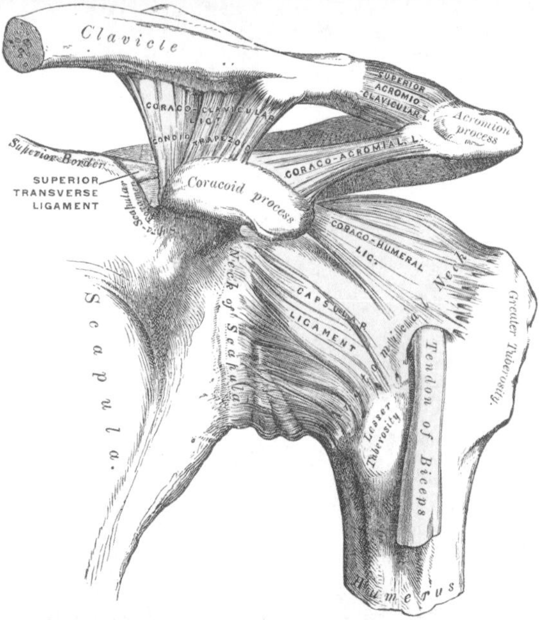

The anatomical illustrations show the shoulder with labels including:

- Clavicle
- Superior Acromio Clavicular L.
- Coraco Clavicular L.
- Acromion Process
- Conoid Ligament
- Trapezoid
- Coraco-Acromial L.
- Superior Border
- Superior Transverse Ligament
- Coracoid Process
- Coraco-Humeral Lig.
- Neck of Scapula
- Capsular Ligament
- Scapula
- Lesser Tuberosity
- Greater Tuberosity
- Tendon of Biceps
- Humerus

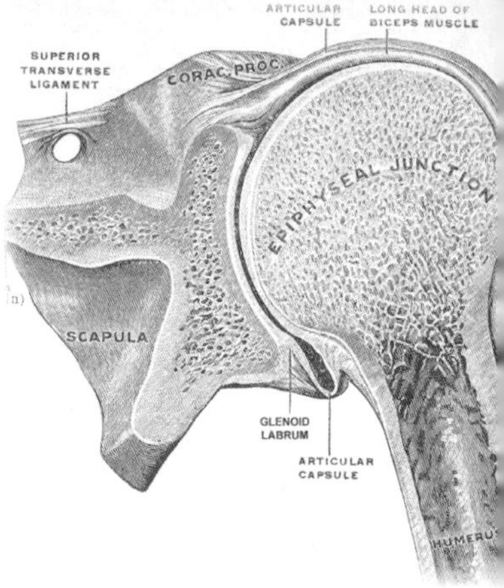

- Superior Transverse Ligament
- Corac. Proc.
- Articular Capsule
- Long Head of Biceps Muscle
- Epiphyseal Junction
- Scapula
- Glenoid Labrum
- Articular Capsule
- Humerus

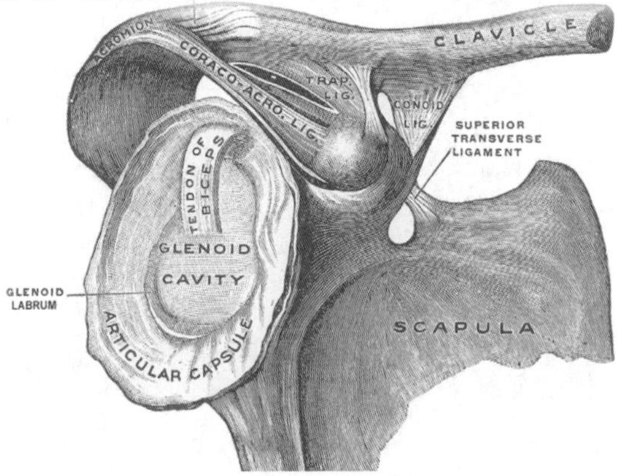

- Acromion
- Coraco-Acro-Lig.
- Trap. Lig.
- Conoid Lig.
- Clavicle
- Superior Transverse Ligament
- Tendon of Biceps
- Glenoid Cavity
- Glenoid Labrum
- Articular Capsule
- Scapula

CHEST AND TRICEP ACTIVATION DURING DIFFERENT PUSHUP VARIATIONS

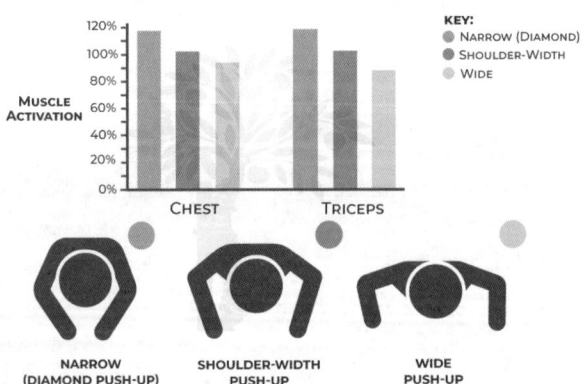

KEY:
- Narrow (Diamond)
- Shoulder-Width
- Wide

Muscle Activation — 120% 100% 80% 60% 40% 20% 0%

CHEST   TRICEPS

NARROW (DIAMOND PUSH-UP)   SHOULDER-WIDTH PUSH-UP   WIDE PUSH-UP

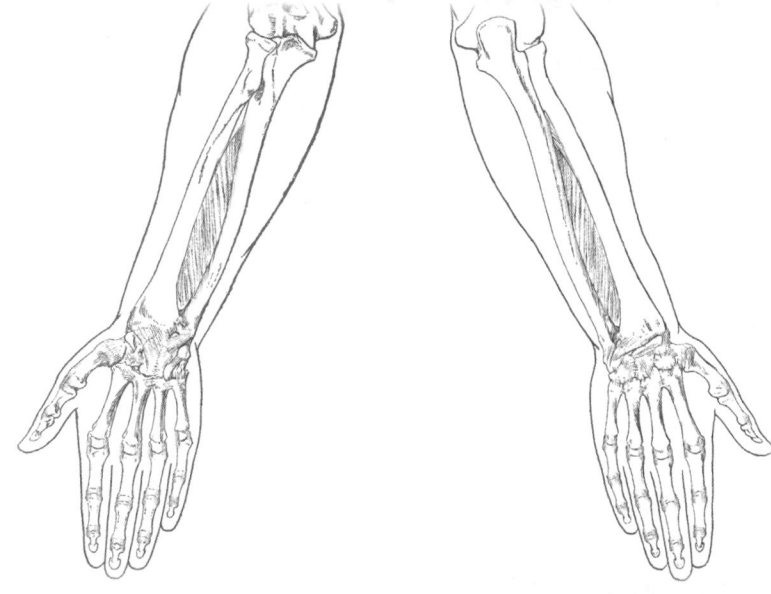

Clinical Note

Carpal tunnel syndrome is due to median nerve entrapment
(see median nerve in Neurovascular chapter)

Carpal Tunnel

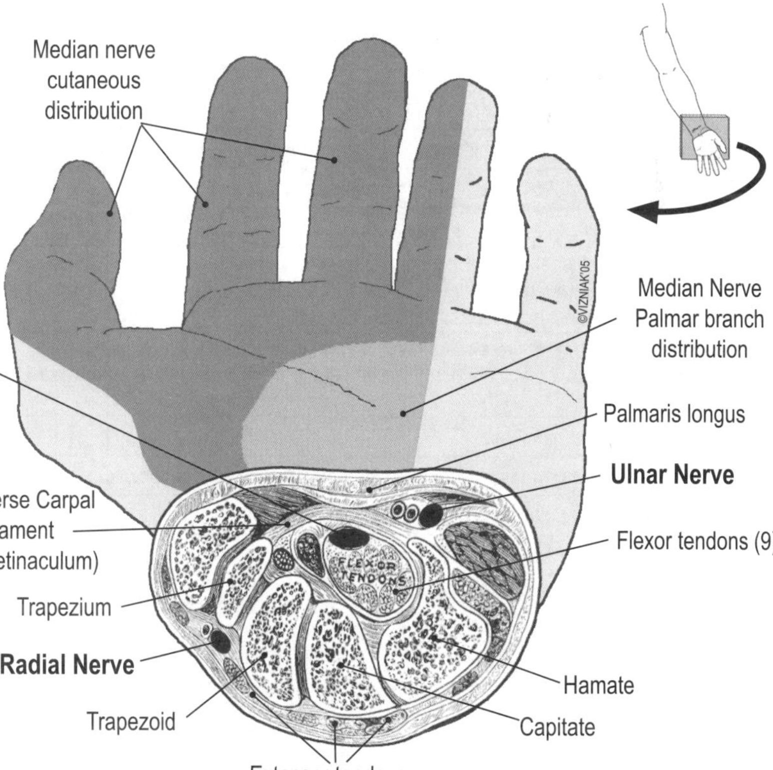

Median nerve
cutaneous
distribution

**Median
Nerve**

Median Nerve
Palmar branch
distribution

Palmaris longus

Ulnar Nerve

Transverse Carpal
Ligament
(flexor retinaculum)

Flexor tendons (9)

Trapezium

Radial Nerve

Hamate

Trapezoid

Capitate

Extensor tendons

©VIZNIAK'05

FLEXOR
TENDONS

prohealthsys

Please rate your ability to do the following activities in the last week by circling the number below the appropriate response.

	difficulty level: none	mild	mod	extreme
1. Open a tight or new jar.	0	1	2	3	4
2. Write.	0	1	2	3	4
3. Turn a key.	0	1	2	3	4
4. Prepare a meal.	0	1	2	3	4
5. Push open a heavy door.	0	1	2	3	4
6. Place an object on a shelf above your head.	0	1	2	3	4
7. Do heavy household chores (e.g., wash walls, wash floors).	0	1	2	3	4
8. Garden or do yard work.	0	1	2	3	4
9. Make a bed.	0	1	2	3	4
10. Carry a shopping bag or briefcase.	0	1	2	3	4
11. Carry a heavy object (over 10 lbs).	0	1	2	3	4
12. Change a lightbulb overhead.	0	1	2	3	4
13. Wash or blow dry your hair.	0	1	2	3	4
14. Wash your back.	0	1	2	3	4
15. Put on a pullover sweater.	0	1	2	3	4
16. Use a knife to cut food.	0	1	2	3	4
17. Recreational activities which require little effort (e.g., cardplaying).	0	1	2	3	4
18. Recreational activities in which you take some force or impact through your arm, shoulder or hand (e.g., golf, hammering, tennis, etc.).	0	1	2	3	4
19. Recreational activities in which you move your arm freely.	0	1	2	3	4
20. Manage transportation needs (getting from one place to another).	0	1	2	3	4
21. Sexual activities.	0	1	2	3	4
22. During the past week, to what extent has your arm, shoulder or hand problem interfered with your normal social activities with family, friends, neighbours or groups?	0	1	2	3	4
23. During the past week, were you limited in your work or other regular daily activities as a result of your arm, shoulder or hand problem? (circle number)	0	1	2	3	4
24. Arm, shoulder or hand pain.	0	1	2	3	4
25. Arm, shoulder or hand pain when you performed any specific activity.	0	1	2	3	4
26. Tingling (pins and needles) in your arm, shoulder or hand.	0	1	2	3	4
27. Weakness in your arm, shoulder or hand.	0	1	2	3	4
28. Stiffness in your arm, shoulder or hand.	0	1	2	3	4
29. During the past week, how much difficulty have you had sleeping because of the pain in your arm, shoulder or hand?	0	1	2	3	4
30. I feel less capable, less confident or less useful because of my arm, shoulder or hand problem.	0	1	2	3	4
COLUMN TOTALS				

Assessment

Upper Body Regional Exam
☑ Check normal, circle & describe abnormal

CC & significant history: _____

Patient: _____ date: _____ (dd/mm/yr)
Insurance: _____

Fracture screen (□ tuning fork, □ percussion, □ torsion test): □ **WNL,** □ **Refer for imaging:** _____
Reflexes: □ **WNL,** □ biceps (C5), □ brachioradialis (C6), □ triceps (C7): _____

Cervicothoracic:
Inspection □ WNL
- □ Posture:
- □ Skin:
- □ Swelling:
- □ Asymmetry:

Palpation: □ WNL
- □ Soft tissue:
- □ Bone:
- □ Lymph nodes:
- □ Pain:

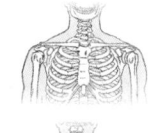

C-ROM	L -act.- R	L -pas- R	L -res.- R	Orthoneuro	L	R
Flexion (50°)				Vaslsalva		
Extension (60°)				Cervical compress.		
Lateral flexion (45°)				Max. compression		
Rotation (80°)				Cervical distraction		
Temporomandibular joint				Soto Hall		
Depres./elevation				Shoulder depression		
Lateral deviation				Adson's		
				Wright's		
				Roo's		

Shoulder:
Inspection □ WNL
- □ Posture:
- □ Skin:
- □ Swelling:
- □ Asymmetry:
- □ Step defect:

Palpation: □ WNL
- □ Soft tissue:
- □ Bone:
- □ Brachial pulse:
- □ Pain:

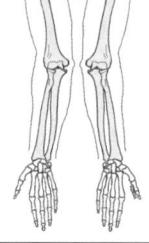

ROM/joint play	L -act.- R	L -pas- R	L -res.- R	Orthoneuro	L	R
Flexion (180°)				Apley sup./inf.		
Extension (50°)				Empty can		
Abduction (180°)				Ant. apprehension		
Adduction (30°)				Faegan's		
Internal rotation (90°)				Hawkins-Kennedy		
External rotation (80°)				Yergason's		
Scapulocostal rhythm:				Speeds		
				Clunk/crank		
				O'Brien		

Elbow:
Inspection □ WNL
- □ Skin:
- □ Swelling:
- □ Asymmetry:

Palpation: □ WNL
- □ Soft tissue:
- □ Bone:
- □ Olecranon bursa:
- □ Pain:

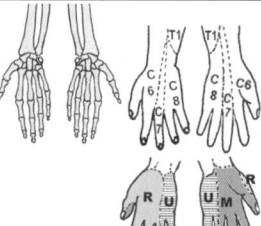

ROM/joint play	L -act.- R	L -pas- R	L -res.- R	Orthoneuro	L	R
Flexion (150°)				Valgus stress		
Extension (0°)				Varus stress		
Supination (90°)				Cozen's		
Pronation (90°)				Mill's		
Other joint play				Book lift test		
Ulnohumeral				Reverse Cozen's		
Radiohumeral				Reverse Mill's		
Proximal radioulnar				Pronator stretch		
				Tinel's (ulnar n.)		

Wrist/hand:
Inspection □ WNL
- □ Skin:
- □ Swelling:
- □ Asymmetry:

Palpation: □ WNL
- □ Soft tissue:
- □ Bone:
- □ Radial pulse:
- □ Ulnar pulse:
- □ Pain:

Wrist ROM	L -act.- R	L -pas- R	L -res.- R	Orthoneuro	L	R
Flexion (80°)				Phalen's (median)		
Extension (70°)				Wrist drop (radial)		
Ulnar flexion (30°)				Froment's (ulnar)		
Radial flexion (20°)				Scaphoid fracture		
Finger flex./ext.				Bracelet		
Finger add./abd.				Thumb abd. stress		
Carpal ROM				Thumb grind		
Grip strength				Finklestein's		
				Tinel's at wrist x 2		

This form is a comprehensive checklist of examination procedures. Each item should be utilized as a diagnostic option based on the patient's presenting symptoms and the clinical discretion of the examiner. Every procedure does not have to be performed on every patient. Some procedures may be contraindicated in certain situations. Patient information contained within this form is considered strictly confidential. Reproduction is permitted for personal use, not for resale or redistribution. www.prohealthsys.com ©Professional Health Systems Inc. All rights reserved. "Dedicated to Clinical Excellence."

Signature: _____ Date: _____

Assessment

prohealthsys

Assessment

Are you getting better? Outcome markers are used to monitor treatment progression. **Any parameter that can be objectively measured has the potential to become a clinical outcome marker.** Listed below are some common outcome markers:

Activities of Daily Living (ADLs)

- The **best functional outcome measure**
- Walking, sitting, chewing food, range of motion
- Ability to perform specific tasks for time
- Playing sports, hobbies, intercourse
- Days of missed work in a set time frame

Pain (subjective)

- **Visual analogue scale (VAS)**
- Verbal pain scale (0-10)
- **Medication or botanical use & dosage (decreased intake is a good thing)**
- Centralization of symptoms, duration, frequency

Flexibility (ROM)

- Global range of motion (AROM, PROM)
- Touch toes (measure finger distance from floor)
- Inclinometer, goniometer, posture chart

Strength

- **Muscle grading (0-5)**
- **Ability to lift weight (kg/ lbs & number of reps)**
- Dynamometer, grip strength (image below)

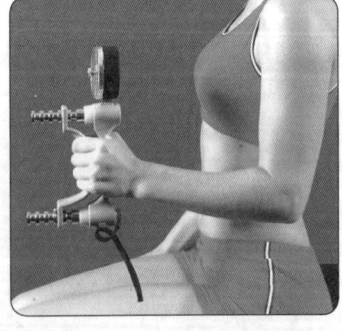

Endurance

- **Walk/run set distance (meters, km)**
- **Back extension repetition, sit-ups**
- **Ability to maintain position (muscle testing)**

Neurological

- Normalization of DTR's, loss of pathologic reflexes
- **Centralization of symptoms** - decreased sensory deficits, muscle strength (dynamometer)
- Improvement on nerve conduction studies

Quality of Life

- **People that report a lower quality of life may be predisposed to poor treatment outcomes**
- "Think of the last week, how would you rate your quality of life?" - excellent, very good, moderate, bad, very bad

Orthopedic tests / Range of Motion

- Active & passive motion before symptoms, utilizing a goniometer, inclinometer
- Change in response to provocative testing

Outcome Assessment Questionnaires

- While Questionnaires show good reliability many patients find it time consuming & somewhat inconvenient to repeatedly fill out multipage forms prior to each treatment
- Oswestry Low Back Pain Disability Questionnaire
- Roland/Morris Disability Questionnaire
- Pain Disability Index

 **30+ Questionnaires on proCentral**

Definition of pain: **an unpleasant sensory and emotional experience associated with actual or potential tissue damage.**[15]

Like an alarm, the point of pain is to get you to do something, often to protect yourself and to create action. Chronic long term pain can even increase the sensitivity to non-injurious stimuli.

Pain is multidimensional long term becomes much more about triggers of sensitivity than about damage or nociception from the tissue. **Doing meaningful activities, building a tolerance to those activities can lead to habituation and less pain.**

Application: **"rate current pain on a scale from 0-10, 0 being no pain, 10 being totally incapacitated."**

1. **Ask separate questions**
   - What is your current pain?
   - What is the pain at its worst? (triggers?)
   - **What is the pain at its least?** (associate activities with least pain & do more of this)

2. Tissue sensitivity to pain

Least sensitive

- Fibrocartilage
- Articular cartilage
- Synovium

- Cortical bone
- Muscle
- Fascia

- Tendons
- Ligaments
- Subchondral bone

Most sensitive

- Fibrous capsule
- Periosteum
- Skin

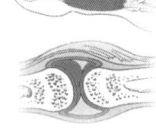

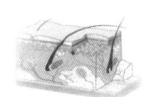

3. **Chronic pain cases**
   - Consider recording the "least pain" the patient has been experiencing (research suggests patients recall "least pain" more accurately than "usual or worst")

4. **Measuring symptoms other than pain**
   - 0-10 scale can be applied to different symptoms (discomfort, nausea, fatigue, stress)

'Pain should be respected, but challenged'
For most rehab., a low amount of pain is OK
up to a 3/10 is usually a safe place to work

If pain is sharp or stops your breath then it is too much - look for the joyful discomfort ☺

Numeric Rating Scale (NRS)

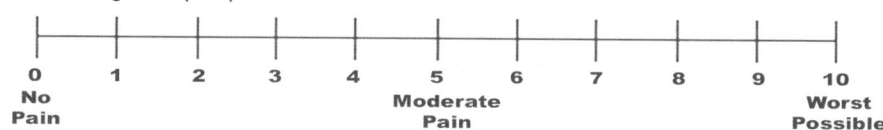

| 0 | 1 | 2 | 3 | 4 | 5 | 6 | 7 | 8 | 9 | 10 |

0 No Pain   **5 Moderate Pain**   **10 Worst Possible**

Faces Pain Scale (as used on ProHealth Goniometer & Posture wall chart)

| Alert smiling | Serious face CAN BE IGNORED | Furrowed brow INTERFERES WITH TASKS | Raised upper lip INTERFERES WITH CONCENTRATION | Slow blink INTERFERES WITH BASIC NEEDS | Moaning - crying BEDREST - REQUIRED |

NO PAIN   **Totally Incapacitated**

Assessment

There is no such thing as perfect posture - through movement, transient stillness and anatomical variation there is always a state of dynamic balance. It can be useful to **observe a patient in standing, seated or in work positions** (especially office workers) or in the stance they spend most of their day (cashiers, machinist) - It is also smart to evaluate **sleeping positions and habits.**

Postures are used to perform activities with the least amount of energy and we can hold a variety of postures for a long period of time. Postural relationships of body parts can be altered/controlled voluntarily, but such control is short-lived because it requires concentration; long-term changes are more difficult.

When discomfort sets in from joint compression, ligamentous tension, continuous muscle contraction (fatigue) or circulatory occlusion (hypooxia) we typically move and stretch our joints and muscles as we settle into a new posture - **the body is designed to move - 'move it or lose it' makes clinical sense!**

Changing posture habits long term requires:
- Increases in ROM (mobilization)
- Stability (if unstable or weak)
- Muscle strength/endurance
- Training (neuronal programming in both proprioception and motor activity = YOGA)

Long term postures without position change can lead to decreased ROM (atrophy/contracture), deformity (slow strains/creep), tissue damage and hypoxia (ulcers/amputation in severe cases)

Teacher Tip: Consider having a section of wall painted with a grid for more accurate postural and AROM assessment - posture exam form and Evidence Based Posture Assessment Chart at prohealthsys.com

| Attention! Military spine | Sway Back | Base Drum Pregnancy | 'Normal' Posture | The Duck | Head Start | Kyphotic Lordotic |

'Tech Neck' aka Computer Spine

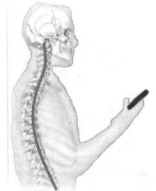 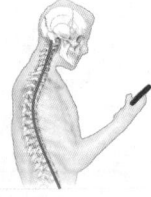 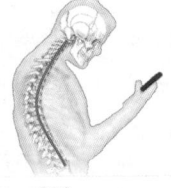 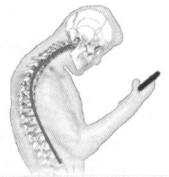 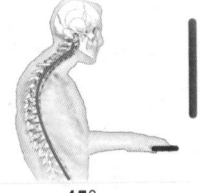

| Neutral - 0° ~10 lbs (4.5kg) | 15° ~27 lbs (12kg) | 30° ~40 lbs (18kg) | 60° ~60 lbs (27kg) | 45° ~49 lbs (22kg) |

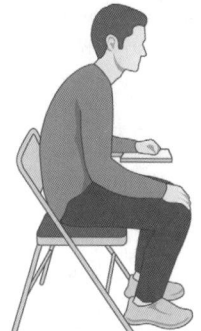

stretching strap to improve posture

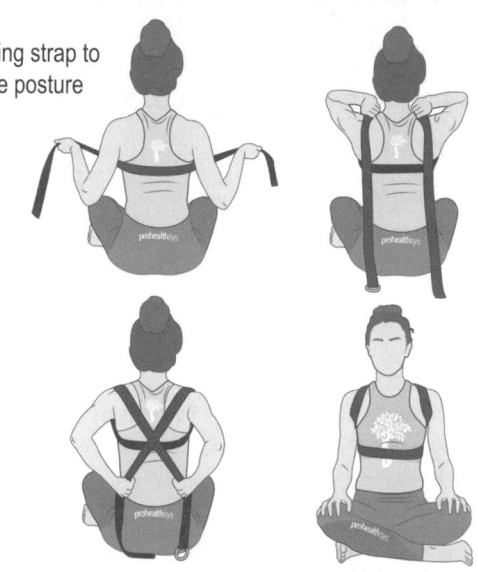

Student Standard / 'Office Express'
- Upper cross syndrome (chin poked, scapulae protracted, thorax in flexion, arms int. rot.)
- Shallow breath cycle

Limit all types of screen time and have **consistent changes of body position** through the entire day - **(sitting < 3 hrs/day increases life expectancy by ~2 years).** Prolonged sedentary time is independently associated with negative health outcomes regardless of physical activity! **Sitting disease = prolonged sitting is the new smoking.** Average North American: 13 hrs/day sitting (computer, driving, phone, eating) + 8 hrs/day lying (sleep, lounging) = ~21 hrs/day of inactivity

(Aviroop, B. et. al. Sedentary Time and Its Association With Risk for Disease Incidence, Mortality, and Hospitalization in Adults: A Systematic Review and Meta-analysis. Annals of Internal Medicine. Jan, 2015.)

Dangers of Prolonged Sitting

- Brain fog & depression
- Neck strain & headaches
- Shoulder & back pain
- Heart disease
- Diabetes& organ issues
- Week core
- Low back pain
- Colon cancer
- Tight hips
- Soft glutes
- Osteoporosis
- Weak leg muscles
- Varicose veins
- Calf & achilies issues

Assessment

Compare bilaterally, examiner should make an introduction statement:
"Try and move as far as possible, if any of the actions or movements are painful or uncomfortable please let me know, do not do any action you feel will cause you further injury."

Flexion (160°-180°)
Muscles Activated: deltoid (anterior fibers), biceps brachii, pectoralis major & coracobrachialis (1st 60° only)
Tissue Stretched: latissimus dorsi, teres major, pectoralis major (lower fibers), triceps brachii (long head), inferior GH capsule, conoid ligament
Tissue Compressed: supraspinatus tendon, subdeltoid bursa, upper GH joint capsule

Extension (40°-60°)
Muscles Activated: deltoid (posterior fibers), latissimus dorsi, teres major/minor, infraspinatus, triceps brachii
Tissue Stretched: deltoid (anterior fibers), biceps brachii, pectoralis major, anterior GH capsule
Tissue Compressed: posterior GH capsule

Abduction (160°-180°)
Muscles Activated: supraspinatus, deltoid (middle fibers), trapezius, serratus anterior
Tissue Stretched: latissimus dorsi, teres major, pectoralis major (lower fibers), triceps brachii (long head), inferior GH capsule, conoid ligament
Tissue Compressed: supraspinatus tendon, subdeltoid bursa, upper GH joint capsule

Adduction (30°-40°)*
Muscles Activated: deltoid (anterior fibers), pectoralis major, latissimus dorsi, teres major, coracobrachialis, trapezius
Tissue Stretched: deltoid (middle fibers), posterior GH capsule
Tissue Compressed: pectoralis major, AC & SC joint, anterior GH capsule

Lateral Rotation (80°-100°)**
Muscles Activated: infraspinatus, teres minor, posterior deltoid
Tissue Stretched: pectoralis major, subscapularis, anterior GH capsule
Tissue Compressed: posterior GH capsule

Medial Rotation (70°-90°)**
Muscles Activated: pec major, subscapularis, anterior deltoid, teres major, latissimus dorsi
Tissue Stretched: infraspinatus, teres minor, posterior deltoid posterior GH capsule
Tissue Compressed: anterior GH capsule

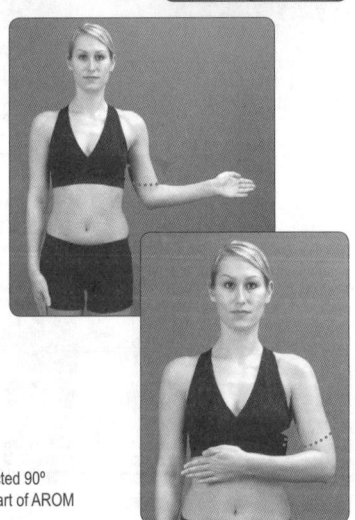

*Adduction may also be assessed with the patient moving the arm behind their back
**Medial & lateral rotation should be tested with the shoulder in neutral & again abducted 90°
Horizontal adduction & abduction & scapular movements may also be assessed as part of AROM

Compare bilaterally; if possible palpate joint during PROM & use the shortest lever possible, start with unaffected; apply over pressure at end ROM; introduction statement: "If any of the actions or movements are painful or uncomfortable please let me know."

Flexion (> 160°-180°)
Tissue Stretched: latissimus dorsi, teres major, pectoralis major (lower fibers), triceps brachii (long head), inferior GH capsule, conoid ligament
Tissue Compressed: supraspinatus tendon, subdeltoid bursa, upper GH joint capsule

Extension (> 40°-60°)
Tissue Stretched: deltoid (anterior fibers), biceps brachii, pectoralis major, anterior GH capsule
Tissue Compressed: posterior GH capsule

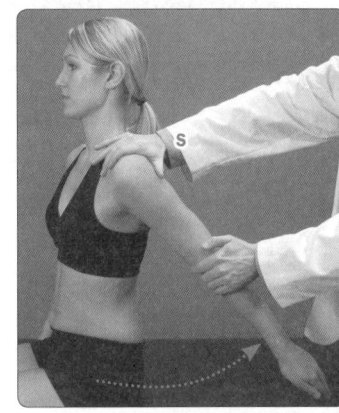

Abduction (> 160°-180°)
Tissue Stretched: latissimus dorsi, teres major, pectoralis major (lower fibers), triceps brachii (long head), inferior GH capsule, conoid ligament
Tissue Compressed: supraspinatus tendon, subdeltoid bursa, upper GH joint capsule

Adduction (> 30°-40°)
Tissue Stretched: deltoid (middle fibers), posterior GH capsule
Tissue Compressed: pectoralis major, AC & SC joint, anterior GH capsule

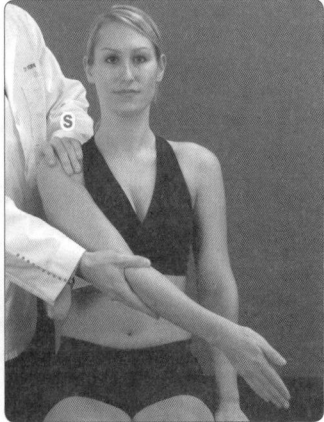

Medial Rotation (> 70°-90°)
Tissue Stretched: infraspinatus, teres minor, posterior deltoid posterior GH capsule
Tissue Compressed: anterior GH capsule

Lateral Rotation (> 80°-100°)
Tissue Stretched: pectoralis major, subscapularis, anterior GH capsule
Tissue Compressed: posterior GH capsule

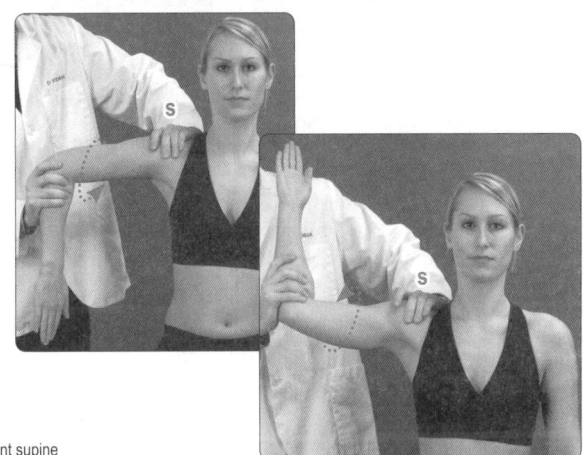

*shoulder PROM may also be assessed with the patient supine

Assessment

Assessment

Compare bilaterally, start with unaffected side for PROM & MMT
Prior to assessing ROM the examiner should make an introduction statement:
"Try and move as far as possible, if any of the actions or movements are painful or uncomfortable please let me know, do not do any action you feel will cause you further injury."

AROM

Flexion (75°-90°)
Muscles Activated: flexor carpi radialis & flexor carpi ulnaris, palmaris longus, flexor digitorum superficialis & profundus
Tissue Stretched: extensor carpi radialis longus & brevis, extensor carpi ulnaris, extensor digitorum, posterior carpal ligaments
Tissue Compressed: carpal tunnel & median nerve

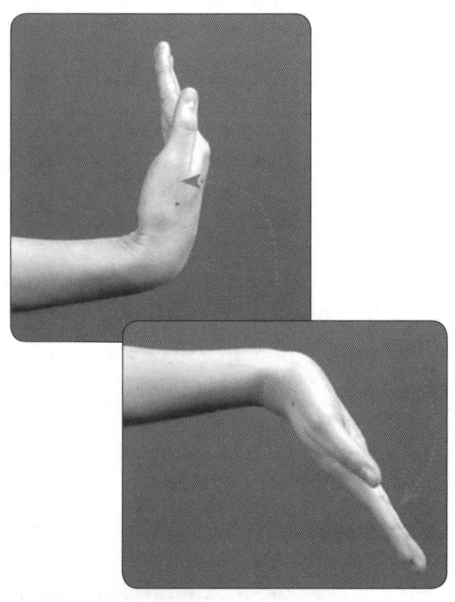

Extension (70°-90°)
Muscles Activated: extensor carpi radialis longus & brevis, extensor carpi ulnaris, extensor digitorum
Tissue Stretched: flexor carpi radialis & flexor carpi ulnaris, palmaris longus, flexor digitorum superficialis & profundus
Tissue Compressed: posterior carpal ligaments

Abduction (radial flexion) (15°-25°)
Muscles Activated: extensor carpi radialis longus/ brevis, flexor carpi radialis
Tissue Stretched: flexor & extensor carpi ulnaris, medial carpal ligament, triangular fibrocartilage
Tissue Compressed: lateral carpal ligaments, scaphoid & trapezium

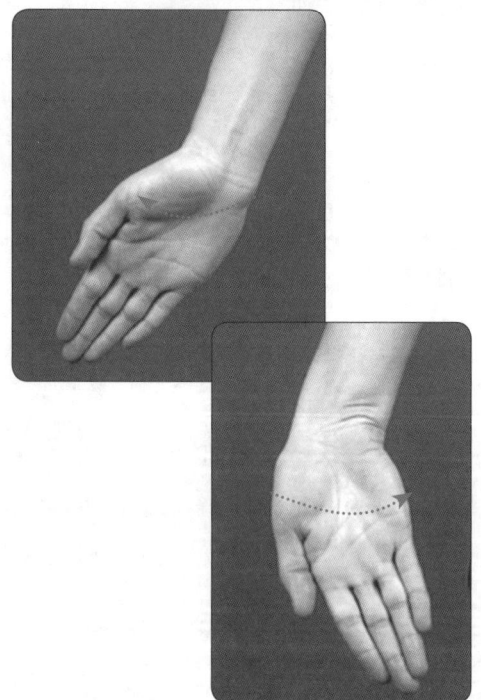

Adduction (ulnar flexion) (20°-35°)
Muscles Activated: flexor & extensor carpi ulnaris
Tissue Stretched: extensor carpi radialis longus/ brevis, flexor carpi radialis, lateral carpal ligaments
Tissue Compressed: medial carpal ligaments, hamate & triquetrum, TFC

prohealthsys

PROM

Flexion (> 150°-160°)
Tissue Stretched: triceps brachii, posterior elbow joint capsule, ulnar nerve
Tissue Compressed: forearm flexors, median nerve, anterior joint capsule

Extension (> 0° to -5°)
Tissue Stretched: brachialis, biceps brachii, brachioradialis, median nerve
Tissue Compressed: posterior joint capsule

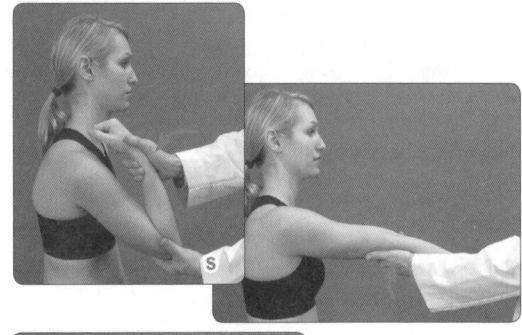

Supination (> 80°-100°)
Tissue Stretched: pronator teres, pronator quadratus
Tissue Compressed:

Pronation (> 80°-100°)
Tissue Stretched: biceps brachii, supinator, brachioradialis
Tissue Compressed:

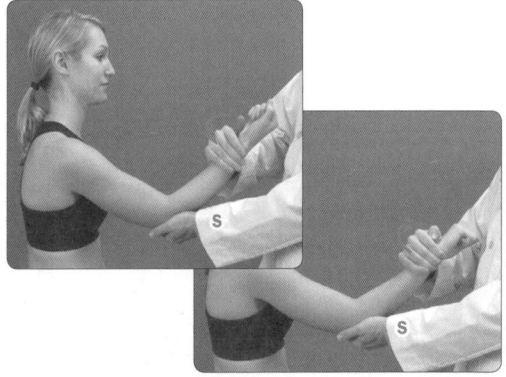

Elbow Muscle Testing

Flexion
Muscles Activated: brachialis, biceps brachii, brachioradialis

Extension
Muscles Activated: triceps brachii, anconeus

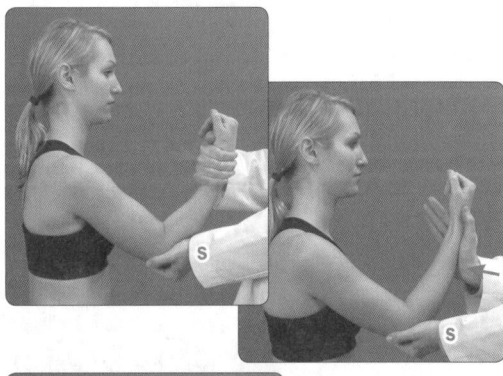

Supination
Muscles Activated: biceps brachii, supinator

Pronation
Muscles Activated: pronator teres, pronator quadratus

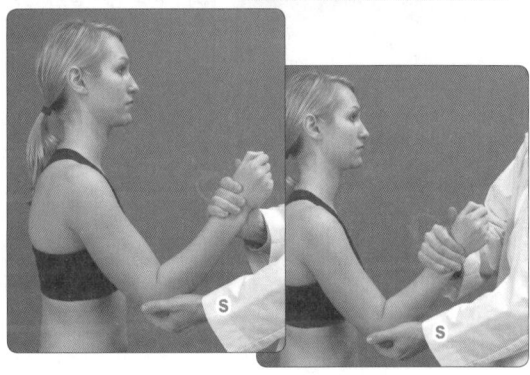

Assessment

prohealthsys

ABCs of Manual Muscle Testing

- **Active Range of Motion (AROM)** - region tested is taken through its full range of motion (establish a baseline of function, warms up muscle capillary beds & neuronal activation)

- **Break test** is a muscle strength test to determine effort exerted by a subject who is performing an **isometric contraction** (examiner applies a **gradual** buildup of pressure to the patient) - apply force along the fiber direction of the muscle (origin to insertion)

- **Concentric Contraction** - patient is asked to perform **concentric AROM** against resistance provided by the examiner (resist enough to **let the patient win**)

- **Stretch** muscle to determine flexibility & length (**PROM** origin away from insertion)

 Video prohealthsys.com

Shoulder Flexion

Muscles Activated: deltoid (anterior fibers), biceps brachii, pectoralis major & coracobrachialis

Shoulder Extension

Muscles Activated: deltoid (posterior fibers), latissimus dorsi, teres major/minor, infraspinatus, triceps brachii

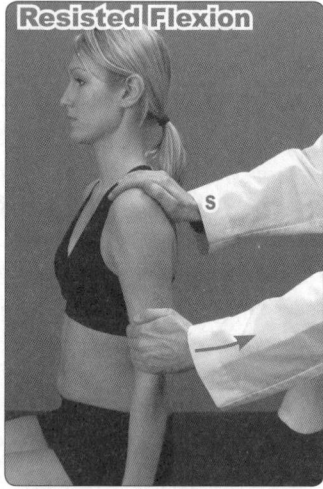
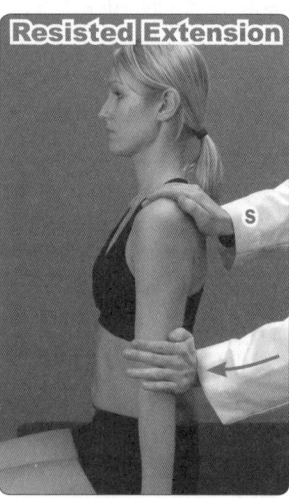

Elbow Flexion

Muscles Activated: brachialis, biceps brachii, brachioradialis

Elbow Extension

Muscles Activated: triceps brachii, anconeus

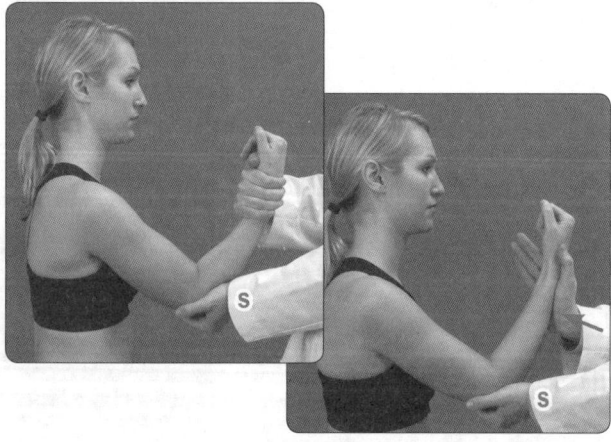

prohealthsys

Common Muscle Testing Findings

- Strong **painless resistance** indicates **normal tissue integrity**

- Weak & painless resistance indicates a loss of motor nerve supply or complete rupture of musculotendinous structure

- **Painful resistance** indicates **partial tear** or rupture of myofascial structure

- 'There is no muscle strength without nerve strength & desire to perform' - *Dr. Nikita Vizniak*

Functional Muscle Testing

Grade	Definition
Functional	5 sec hold, 5-6 reps
Fair	3-4 sec hold, 2-4 reps
Poor	1-2 sec hold, 1-2 reps
Non Functional	0 sec, 0 reps

Subscapularis Test

Patient position
- Prone or seated, arm behind lower lumbar spine

Examiner's force
- Straight posterior to anterior (make sure patient lifts arm away from body, not extension of elbow)

Stabilization - none required

Variation: subscapularis may also be tested with pectoralis major by testing the arm into internal rotation (tested in two positions; shoulder at 0° & 90°) - see testing for teres minor/infraspinatus - examiner pushes in opposite direction

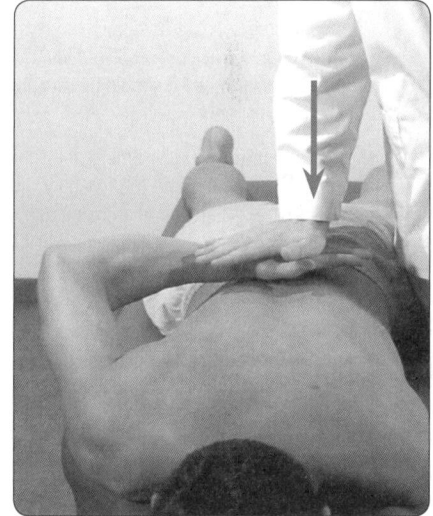

Learn More

MUSCLE MANUAL

Start — Windup — Cocking — Acceleration — Release — Decel. — Follow through

Foot down — Max external rotation & weight transfer forward

Anterior Apprehension Test ★ ★ ★ ★ ★

Procedure

Patient seated or supine, shoulder abducted 90° elbow flexed 90°; examiner gently applies P-A pressure over the humerus & observes patient for signs of apprehension or discomfort (grimace or pulls away)

Interpretation

(+) Excessive anterior translation, dislocation or patient apprehension → anterior GH instability (SN: 53 SP: 99 +LR: 53 -LR: 0.47)[42, 57]

Clinical notes (grades of shoulder instability)

If the test is performed supine, examiner better able to observe patient's face for signs of apprehension

Grade	Description
Normal	0-25% translation
I	25-50% translation, humeral head riding up on glenoid labrum
II	50-75% translation, humeral head rides up & over glenoid labrum, but immediately reduces
III	> 75% translation & humeral head remains dislocated; in cases of severe instability diagnostic imaging should be an immediate follow-up (MRI, x-ray)

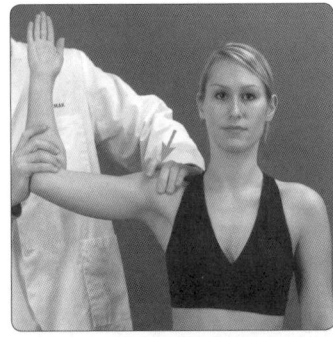

New Pain Provocation Test: examiner may choose to perform apprehension test action with forearm fully supinated & then forearm fully pronated (pronation increases stress on glenoid labrum & may show increase validity to rule in labral pathologies) - (SN: 100 SP: 90)[5]

Empty Can Test ★ ★ ★ ★ ★

Procedure

Patient standing or seated, actively raises straight arm (palm up) to 120° in scaption (scapular) plane; at apex patient internally rotates arm (thumb down "empty can"), then lowers straight arm internally rotated slowly to the body

Interpretation

(+) Pain or weakness → injury or lesion of supraspinatus muscle (SN: 44-89 SP: 50-90 +LR: 1.8-4.2 -LR: 0.22-0.63)[29, 54, 56]

Clinical notes

Refer to scapulohumeral rhythm (page 64-65) for detailed shoulder abduction parameters

Clinician's option: both arms may be done simultaneously & examiner may apply over pressure at the apex of shoulder abduction or during entire motion

Lift-off Test ★★★★★

Procedure - Patient seated, standing or prone, patient rests dorsal surface of hand against sacrum/lumbar spine & attempts to move hand posteriorly; examiner may observe action or apply gentle resistance to motion - make sure the patient is rotating the shoulder & not extending shoulder! (consider stabilizing the elbow)

Interpretation

(+) Inability to lift hand off sacrum → Complete tear or paralysis on subscapularis muscle, subscapularis or rotator cuff lesion, subscapularis MFTP

Clinical notes

The lift off test mainly activates the lower fibers of the subscapularis (bear hug test activates mainly upper fibers) - consider measuring the distance from the patient's spine to the hand to get a quantitative outcome measure to evaluate treatment success

This test appears to be very specific to rule in the presence of a subscapularis tear, but may require ~70% muscle tear for (+) result (R: 0.32 SN: 62-92 SP: 100)[21, 26, 54]

Roo's/EAST Test ★★★★★

Synonym: EAST (elevated arm stress test), Provocative Elevation Test

Procedure

Patient seated, shoulders 90° abducted, elbows flexed 90°, examiner instructs patient to open & close fists ~2x/sec for 3 minutes

Interpretation

(+) Inability to maintain action with associated numbness, tingling or weakness → TOS (SN: 82 SP: 100)[5, 12]

Clinical notes

Clinically 3 minute duration may not be required, typically one minute is usually enough time for patients to exhibit symptoms of TOS

Test may demonstrate many false positives (~47% in normal population)

Assessment

Cozen's Test ★★★★

Procedure

Patient seated, elbow fully flexed, forearm pronated & wrist extended ("waiter position"); examiner applies force in the direction of elbow extension & wrist flexion while stabilizing the patient's elbow with the other hand

May be done as an isometric test (1) or as a exxentric contraction test (2)

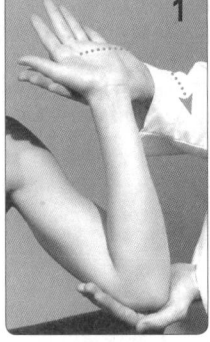

Interpretation

(+) Pain or weakness → lateral epicondylitis

Clinical notes

Patients often describe pain felt with this test as sharp & shooting, this pain may also be reproduced with palpation over the radial nerve & common extensor tendon

Examiner may also individually muscle test extensor carpi radialis longus & brevis muscles

Mill's Test ★★★★

Procedure

Patient seated, examiner extends & pronates patient's elbow while flexing the wrist (test stretches the common extensor tendon)

Interpretation

(+) Lateral elbow pain during test → lateral epicondylitis

Clinical notes

Clinician's option: consider flexing the fingers & applying pressure with your thumb over the common extensor tendon to further increase the sensitivity of this test

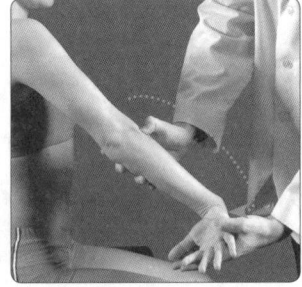

Mill's test may be used as a treatment for lateral epicondylitis (stretching of the common extensor tendon)

Tinel's Sign at Elbow ★★★★

Synonym: distal tingling on percussion (DTP) sign

Procedure

Patient seated, examiner gently taps 4-6 times over cubital tunnel (groove between the olecranon process & medial epicondyle) with fingertips or reflex hammer

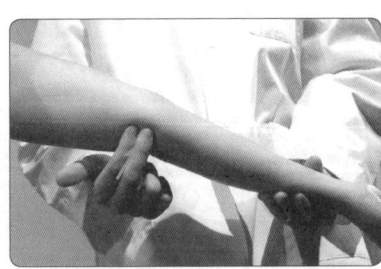

Interpretation

(+) Shooting electrical pain along the medial side of the forearm to medial hand → ulnar compressive neuropathy

Clinical notes

This test demonstrates a high rate of false positives with asymptomatic elbows; hitting your "funny bone" is really rapid compression of the ulnar nerve at this location. (SN: 70 SP: 98 +LR: 35 -LR: 0.31)[61]

prohealthsys

Phalen's Test ★★★★★

Procedure

Patient seated with wrists maximally flexed, two versions:
1. Patient places back of hands together in front of body so both wrists are fully flexed & maintains position for up to 1 minute
2. Examiner gently holds involve wrist in sustained flexion position for 1 minute

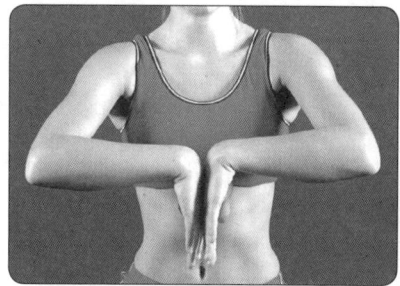

Interpretation

(+) Numbness or tingling over the distribution of the median nerve, increased anterior wrist pain or subsequent weakness of thumb opposition → carpal tunnel syndrome (R: 0.79 SN: 10-88 SP: 33-100 +LR: 0.7-41.5 -LR: 0.1-1)[5, 13, 17, 18, 20, 27, 24, 31, 33, 35, 37, 38, 39, 41, 42, 46, 51, 53, 59, 60,64, 68, 74, 79, 80, 83, 87, 88]

Assessment

Finklestein's Test ★★★★★

Procedure - Patient seated or standing makes fist with thumb inside fingers & ulnar deviates the wrist; patient may actively move wrist or examiner may passively move wrist

Interpretation

(+) Pain on lateral wrist → tenosynovitis of the abductor pollicis longus & extensor pollicis brevis tendons (De Quervain's disease)

Clinical notes

Test may be performed actively by patient or passively by examiner

Pain is often described as "exquisite, sharp & localized"

False-positive Finkelstein test can result from 1st mcp joint pathology (SN: 81 SP: 50 +LR: 1.6 -LR: 0.38)[12, 32]

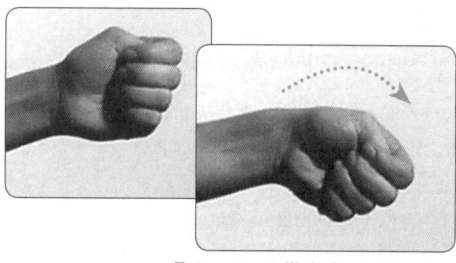

Extensor pollicis longus

Extensor pollicis brevis

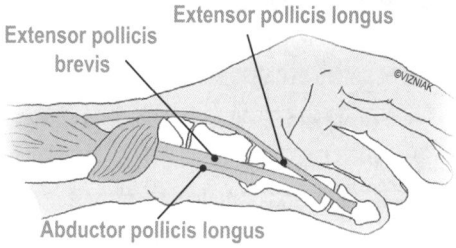

Abductor pollicis longus

©VIZNIAK

Definition

Vladimir Janda, a Czechoslovakian neurologist & physiatrist (MD), advocated **structural & functional assessment** applications in musculoskeletal medicine. The structural approach relates pain and/or dysfunction with the pathology of specific static structures, which works well for acute conditions with easily visible tissue damage. The functional approach recognizes the function of processes & systems within the body, **rather than focusing on a single site of pathology**, which works better for the diagnosis & treatment of chronic conditions & functional rehabilitation.

The Janda approach to chronic pain emphasizes muscle function. By observing **muscle firing patterns** during specific body motions clinicians are able to note imbalances in motion & muscle contraction, the normal patterns are known as key or functional movement patterns (FMP), deviation from normal limits suggest compensation or muscle imbalance.

Observation

1. Observe FMP visually
2. Observe FMP through palpation (especially if visual observation is inconclusive)
3. Know your anatomy (agonists, antagonists, synergists, stabilizers)
4. Investigate abnormal FMP by evaluating list of potential causes
   - Local biomechanical and/or regional problems
   - Postural and/or regional problems
   - Biomechanical problems away from the FMP area (compensation)
   - Tight antagonist(s)
   - Tight/overactive synergist(s)
   - Tight/overactive stabilizer(s)
   - Slow proprioceptive ("sleepy") agonist
   - Weak agonist
5. Evaluate all above potential causes one after another & record findings
6. CORRECTIONS: After evaluation of all potential causes, start with patient goals, then biomechanical abnormalities & apply therapy. Check FMP after therapy before moving on to the next.

Clinician teaching sequence

1. Clinician describes to patient what is to be done
2. Clinician demonstrates to the patient what is to be done
3. Patient demonstrates to clinician how it is done
4. Clinician monitors patient's progress by observing how patient performs activity on subsequent visits

Home care

1. Give patient specific stretches or strengthening exercises (tracks)
2. Give patient posture exercises when needed
3. Once FMP starts improving give patient mental & proprioceptive retraining exercises – to practice FMP through whatever range of motion they can perform while maintaining proper movement form/pattern
4. Teach friend/spouse/care giver how to help patient by monitoring FMP

Altered scapulohumeral rhythm
- Weak agonist: lower & middle trapezius
- Overactive synergist: upper trapezius, levator scapulae & rhomboids

Symptoms related to altered scapulohumeral rhythm
- Neck pain, headaches, thoracic pain
- Rotator cuff syndromes (i.e. impingement syndrome)
- Shoulder blade pain

Evaluation
- Patient is seated with elbow flexed to 90° to limit unwanted rotation
- Patient is instructed to slowly abduct the arms
- (+) test if scapular elevation or rotation (laterally) occurs in first 30° to 60°
- A false (+) can occur if scapula is already elevated & laterally rotated with arms at side

Rationale
- Identify loss of normal glenohumeral rhythm due to over-activity of the upper trapezius &/or levator scapulae muscles

Postural analysis
- Internally rotated shoulders
- Upward rotation of the scapulae
- Hyperkyphosis of thoracic spine (common)

Gait analysis
- Altered arm swing
- Shoulder elevation with arm flexion (shoulder hiking)

Myofascial trigger points
- Upper, mid & low traps; levator scapulae
- Subscapularis
- Mastoid process & C2 & C3 insertion

Mobility (joint dysfunction/subluxation)
- Upper cervical spine
- Cervical-thoracic junction
- Mid thoracic & scapulocostal

Treatment
- Mobilize/adjust neck & cervical-thoracic junction
- Facilitate/strengthen lower & middle traps
- Relax/stretch up traps, levator scapulae & subscapularis
- Breathing correction & ergonomic advice

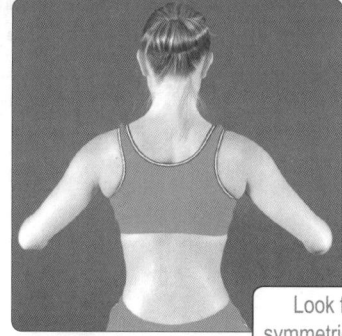
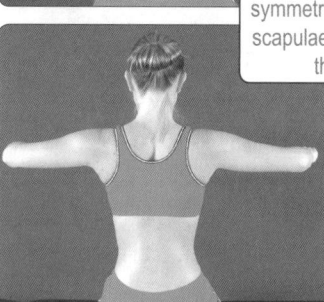

Look for smooth, symmetrical glide of the scapulae & elevation of the arms

Assessment

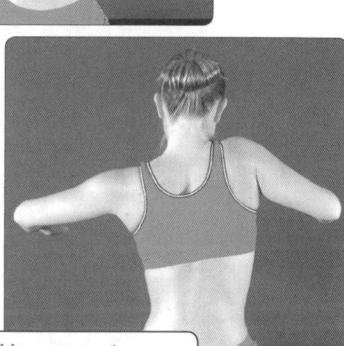

Shoulder hiking suggests an overactive upper trapezius &/or inhibited middle & lower trapezius

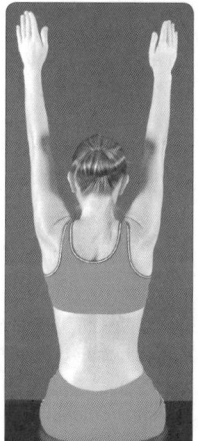

Also watch for winging of the scapula which suggests weak serratus anterior &/or a long thoracic nerve lesion

Elbow	Clinical notes
Lateral epicondylitis	*Hx:* repetitive motions (gripping, hammering, lifting, tennis backhand) *SSx:* tender to palpation over lateral epicondyle/common extensor tendon; ↑ elbow pain with resisted wrist extension; (+) Mill's, Cozen's Test *DDx:* cervical radiculopathy, posterior interosseous nerve entrapment
Medial epicondylitis	*Hx:* repetitive motions (gripping, lifting, golfing) *SSx:* tender to palpation over medial epicondyle/common flexor tendon; ↑ elbow pain with resisted wrist flexion; (+) reverse Mill's, reverse Cozen's Test *DDx:* cervical radiculopathy
Pulled (Toddler's) **Elbow**	*Hx:* child (age 1-4) swung by arms or arm tugged "hurry up Sally" *SSx:* pain & apprehension, child is unwilling to straighten elbow *DDx:* elbow or wrist fracture (usually more significant trauma)
Pronator teres syndrome	*Hx:* repetitive motions (gripping with pronation), tingling & weakness in hand *SSx:* tender to palpation over mid pronator teres; ↑ hand symptoms with palpation of pronator teres, weakness in wrist flexion; (+) Tinel's (possible) *DDx:* cervical radiculopathy, carpal tunnel syndrome - Remember the median nerve travels between the 2 heads of pronator teres

Wrist/Hand	Clinical notes
Carpal tunnel syndrome	*Hx:* insidious onset; paresthesia into hand; loss of digital dexterity *SSx:* (+) Tinel's, Phalen's test; ↓ sensation over median nerve distribution in hand *DDx:* pronator teres syndrome, thoracic outlet syndrome, C6-C7 radiculopathy
de Quervain's tenosynovitis	*Hx:* aching pain above radial styloid; worse with wrist & thumb movements *SSx:* (+) Finkelstein's test; audible squeaking sound with wrist movement *DDx:* scaphoid fracture, osteoarthrosis
Wrist Sprain	*Hx:* traumatic extension or flexion of wrist (FOOSH) *SSx:* palpable tenderness over ligaments, limited AROM & PROM (+) bracelet test *DDx:* scaphoid fracture, TFC tear, rheumatoid or septic arthritis
Ganglion cyst	*Hx:* painful or painless lump or mass on wrist, weight bearing aggravates (push-up) *SSx:* palpable, solid mass, may be tender to palpation *DDx:* infection, carpal subluxation
Lunate dislocation	*Hx:* FOOSH (fall on out stretched hand) or impact trauma to hand *SSx:* tenderness in wrist in line with 3rd metacarpal; visible on x-ray (spilled tea cup) *DDx:* lunate or scaphoid fracture, osteoarthrosis
Scaphoid fracture	*Hx:* FOOSH (fall on out stretched hand) or impact trauma to hand *SSx:* pain in anatomical snuff box with radial flexion; (+) scaphoid fracture test *DDx:* lunate dislocation, osteoarthrosis
TFC Tear	*Hx:* FOOSH (fall on out stretched hand) or impact trauma to hand with twisting *SSx:* local pain with ROM; possible ↓ ROM & grip strength; (+) TFC dorsal glide *DDx:* lunate dislocation, ulnar styloid fracture, osteoarthrosis

↑ = increase, ↓ = decrease, Hx = history, SSx = signs & symptoms, DDx = differential diagnosis, (+) = positive, TFC = triangular fibrocartilage
FOOSH = Fall On Out Stretched Hand - see blue 'Orthopedic Conditions' and yellow 'Physical Assessment' texts for more details

Condition	Clinical notes
AC separation	*Hx:* prior trauma - fall onto shoulder or impact over shoulder *SSx:* possible step defect; tenderness to palpation over AC joint; (+) AC shear, cross-body test, O'Brien's *DDx:* supraspinatus rupture, impingement syndrome, rotator cuff tear
Adhesive capsulitis **(Frozen shoulder)**	*Hx:* patient age 40-60, usually female, weeks of shoulder pain & restriction *SSx:* restricted AROM in clear capsular pattern (external rotation > abduction > internal rotation); extremely painful & limited PROM *DDx:* cervical pathology, impingement syndrome, rotator cuff tear
Bicipital tendonitis	*Hx:* pain over anterior shoulder, history of repetitive elbow flexion (weight lifter) *SSx:* exquisite pain with direct palpation of biceps long head tendon; pain with resisted horizontal adduction *DDx:* cervical pathology, rotator cuff strain
Bursitis (subacromial)	*Hx:* pain over superior or lateral GH joint, pain at night difficulty sleeping *SSx:* tender palpation over acromion/deltoid; ↓ shoulder ROM in abduction & flexion; pain may be relieved by GH inferior distraction *DDx:* cervical pathology, rotator cuff strain, impingement syndrome
Glenoid Labral Tear	*Hx:* usually repetitive shoulder motion, throwing athletes or weight-lifters *SSx:* ↓ shoulder ROM in abduction & flexion; pain may be relieved by GH inferior distraction (+) O'Brien's, clunk or crank test *DDx:* Bicipital Tendonitis, Impingement Syndrome, Rotator Cuff Injury
Glenohumeral osteoarthrosis	*Hx:* insidious onset of pain, morning stiffness, worse with excessive activity *SSx:* crepitus & pain w/ ROM; (+) Ellman compression test (GH scour test) *DDx:* AC osteoarthrosis, GH instability, impingement syndrome
Impingement	*Hx:* pain with overhead movements, may refer pain down lateral arm *SSx:* pain with ROM; (+) painful arc, Hawkin's-Kennedy, Neer's *DDx:* cervical pathology, GH instability, poor posture
Instability	*Hx:* prior trauma; patient may be able to demonstrate ↑ motion; patient may have impingement type symptoms due to excess GH movement *SSx:* observation of sulcus sign; (+) load & shift test *DDx:* rotator cuff strain, impingement syndrome, congenital ligament laxity
Rotator cuff tear	*Hx:* prior trauma - lifting or throwing injury; degeneration of rotator cuff? (elderly) *SSx:* weakness in specific rotator cuff movements, abnormal scapulohumeral rhythm; (+) Codman's arm drop, impingement signs, painful arc *DDx:* supraspinatus rupture, impingement syndrome, congenital ligament laxity
Supraspinatus tendonitis	*Hx:* pain with overhead movements or hand placed behind back *SSx:* exquisite pain with resisted supraspinatus movements; (+) empty can test, impingement, pain with direct palpation *DDx:* cervical pathology, GH instability, complete supraspinatus rupture
Thoracic outlet syndrome	*Hx:* pain & paresthesia, possible muscle weakness into shoulder, arm &/or hand *SSx:* myospasm of cervical musculature (depending on cause); (+) TOS tests *DDx:* cervical radiculopathy, cervical disc herniation, carpal tunnel syndrome

Assessment

↑ = increase, ↓ = decrease, Hx = history, SSx = signs & symptoms, DDx = differential diagnosis
see blue 'Orthopedic Conditions' text for more details

Assessment

Basics

Definition: stretch or tear of the rotator cuff tendon or muscle belly. Grade of strain depends on amount of fibers damaged, degree of pain & strength of muscle contraction. **Give an exact diagnosis of tendons involved as it will change treatment** - do NOT call an isolated subscapularis tear a rotator cuff strain!

Pathophysiology

- **Degenerative strain** - associated with minimal trauma, often prior to chronic tendonitis or chronic impingement syndrome

- **Acute traumatic strain** – can present following a specific trauma (FOOSH, or a single violent blow or force to shoulder). Prolonged or repetitive overuse of muscle/tendon over a short period of time, lifting or pulling. Pre-existing impingement syndrome

Demographics

Incidence: ~30% of population

Age: degenerative type is common in elderly

Gender: male > female

Risk factors: motions that require **repeated overhead motions or forceful pulling** motions. Sports injuries or trauma in athletes making repetitive motions (baseball pitchers, swimmers, quarterbacks, volleyball, boxers, kayaking, tennis)

- Poor nutrition, obesity & reduced strength or flexibility & previous injury

Diagnosis

History

- **Pain over superior lateral shoulder**, aggravated by leaning on elbow & pushing upwards on shoulder. **Popping or tearing sensation at moment of injury**, followed by pain & weakness.

- Edema, erythema and/or hematoma of shoulder, axilla, and/or upper arm (severe case)

- Intolerance to overhead activity

- Pain at night, especially when lying directly on affected shoulder

- Weakness may be reported, but is often masked by pain and is usually found only through examination. With longer standing pain, the opposite shoulder is favored and gradually loss of motion and weakness may develop

- Loss of strength, possible crepitus with motion

Physical

Inspection: normal bone and soft tissue outlines. Protective shoulder hike may be seen. Possible wasting in the supraspinatus and infraspinatus fossae (chronic cases)

Palpation: tenderness over rotator cuff muscles. Myospasm & myofascial trigger points

Motion:

- **AROM:** weakness or pain during abduction, external rotation, internal rotation, or any combination of these actions - depends on which muscle(s) is specifically damaged

- **PROM:** pain if impingement occurs or pain at end-range if muscle is stretches

- **RROM:** pain and weakness during abduction, lateral &/or medial rotation

Differential Diagnosis

- Supraspinatus rupture, Impingement syndrome
- GH ligament laxity or instability, labral tear
- Biceps strain/tendinopathy
- Remember: shoulder pain can be referred from either the chest or abdomen (coronary artery disease, pulmonary tumors, & gallbladder disease)

Special Test

- (+) ↓ ROM with Apley's tests. (+) Codman's Arm Drop; if not severe, apply slight downward pressure at elbow. (+) Empty Can test. (+) Lift off test combined w/ weakness during internal rotation. (+) Weakness during Bear-hug test, Belly press. (+) Internal Rotation lag sign

Empty Can

Diagnostic Imaging

- *Ultrasound:* provides a dynamic assessment of cuff integrity (best initial imaging modality)

- *X-rays:* evaluate bony injury, including a rotator cuff avulsion fracture, subluxation or dislocation

- *MRI:* evaluates co-existing shoulder injuries such as Labral tear & other soft tissue pathologies

Other - Arthroscopy - gold standard investigation, allowing a direct inspection and repair of torn structures in the shoulder joint

Treatment

General Measures - METH - avoid prolong immobilization (increases risk of Frozen shoulder). Avoid actions that cause aggravation. Consider cold application if acute, switch to heat in chronic cases. Avoid premature return to activity - can result in chronic tendinopathy or impingement

Massage Therapy - can be started 2 days to 2 weeks after the injury depending on severity & patient tolerance. Myofascial trigger point therapy, myofascial release & cross fiber, pin & stretch, IASTM

Osseous Mobes/Manipulation - Do not perform on shoulder during acute phase. Initially focus on thoracic & cervical spine then move to shoulder mobes & manip. as tolerated

Electrotherapy - ultrasound - set at a level that produces a mild feeling of warmth (increase local blood flow, help activate cells involved in healing process & speed repair of tissue). Interferential or microcurrent may offer benefit

Acupuncture - LI4, SI3, SJ4, 5 & 6; UB 17, 18, & 19, LV3, GB34, SP10, UB17

Diet & Botanicals - ↑ protein intake to help muscle/tendon heal. Vitamin C, E, selenium, fish oils, Ca, Mg. Anti-inflammatory: *Curcuma longa, Boswellia.* Analgesic: *Salix alba, Filipendula ulmaris.* Vulnerary: *Arnica montana, Symphytum officinale*

Medications - NSAIDs (Aspirin, Ibuprofen). Corticosteroid injection are controversial may lower inflammation may help chronic rotator cuff tear to allow rehabilitation to proceed

Surgery (last resort) - Arthroscopic, open or mini-open repair. After surgical repair ~80% of patients achieve a satisfactory result (adequate pain relief, restoration or improvement of function, improvement in range of motion)

Follow-up

Rehabilitation Program - main goal is elimination of pain & restoration of motion, flexibility, strength & endurance. Initial period of rest (allows adequate healing). Consider short-term use of a sling. Pain free PROM exercises & stretching. Progress to pain free AROM. Consider aquatherapy to add resistance to AROM. Progress to resisted weight exercises & stretching. Then functional activities & ADLs.

Patient Monitoring - begin rehab. as an outpatient therapy, followed by an at-home routine - **be sure to have patient demonstrate exercise routines to ensure proper technique**

Prevention/Patient Education - adequate warm-up prior to sports activity. Wear properly fitted & appropriate protective equipment during contact sports (pads & tape). ***Complete rehabilitation of previous injuries.*** Improve technique, avoid aggravating activities & avoid overuse

Prognosis - early, active intervention is essential for a rapid return to activity or sport. The severity of injury will determine how fast the patient heals
- Grade 1 (mild): 2-4 weeks
- Grade 2 (moderate): 4-12 weeks
- Grade 3 (severe): 3 months-1 year

- *Complications:* Shoulder instability, which can lead to Impingement or Adhesive capsulitis

Medicolegal - workers' compensation claims seemed to play a role in the satisfaction of surgical results ('green back' syndrome)

Single Leg Scarecrow

Wall Push-Up

Assessment

prohealthsys

Basics

Definition: narrowing of space between acromion & humerus that results in 'pinching' of the rotator cuff tendons (esp. supraspinatus) &/or biceps brachii long head

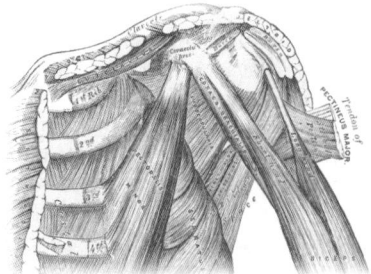

Pathophysiology: (Neer stages)

- *Stage 1:* usually < 25 yrs old - edema & hemorrhage resulting from excessive overhead activities; reversible with conservative treatment
- *Stage 2:* usually 25-40 yrs - tendinopathy resulting from repeated episodes of mechanically induced inflammation; shoulder functions satisfactorily during light activity but becomes symptomatic after vigorous overhead use, excessive repetitive use or heavy lifting; conservative treatment may offer benefit
- *Stage 3:* > 40 yrs - trophic changes in rotator cuff, biceps, & adjacent bone (osteophytes) leading to tendon ruptures & alterations of acromion & greater tuberosity; progressive disability often leads to surgical intervention

Demographics

Incidence: higher in athletes & laborers

Age: 25-40 yrs   *Gender:* male > female (2:1)

Risk factors: prior injury or repeated overhead activities (swimmers, baseball, volleyball, painters, racket sports), GH instability, enlarged acromion or coracoid process

Diagnosis

History

- **Dull achy shoulder pain** that is worse with shoulder abduction above 80°, overhead activity or excessive use. Sudden onset of sharp pain with tearing sensation suggests rotator cuff tear

- Gradual increase in shoulder pain with overhead activities suggests impingement. Pain may be worse after sleep if arm was abducted over head or sleeping on a firm mattress (**ask about sleeping position - very important**)

Physical

Inspection: check muscle atrophy, asymmetry & swelling, warmth, redness

Palpation:

- Pain on top of shoulder → AC joint arthritis
- Pain over bicipital groove → Bicipital tendonitis
- Lateral shoulder → Supraspinatus tendinopathy

Motion: AROM: **painful arc - pain with shoulder abduction or flexion from 80-120° & shoulder hiking on affected side.** Other AROM may be limited above 80°

Painful arc on left shoulder
(note shoulder hike & slower motion)

- *PROM:* usually WNL unless tendon is compressed with passive action (see special tests)
- *RROM:* possible muscle weakness due to pain with muscle tests if there co-existing tears or inflammation

Neurovascular: usually WNL, but need to rule out cervical raduculopathy or other neurologic issues

Differential Diagnosis

- Difficult to diagnosis - similar to other shoulder pathologies that may co-exist. Biceps tendonitis, rotator cuff injuries, adhesive capsulitis, AC joint pathology, glenoid labral tear, bursitis

Special Test (see yellow *Physical Assessment* text)

- (+) Impingement sign (AROM in flexion with palm up then repeated with palm down)
- (+) Neer's test (PROM in flexion with palm up then repeated with palm down)
- (+) Hawkins-Kennedy test causes supraspinatus tendon to impinge against coracoacromial ligamentous arch

- (+) Pain with rotator cuff tests - Drop arm test, Empty can test

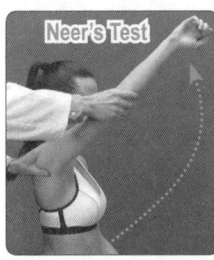

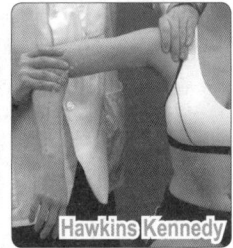

Neer's Test

Hawkins Kennedy

Impingement Sign (palm up then palm down)

Diagnostic Imaging: (usually not indicated)

- *X-rays:* may be indicated to rule out arthritis or other pathologies. *MRI:* best imaging to evaluate soft tissue changes & rule in or out other shoulder pathologies
- **Other -** Impingement test: injection 10 mL of 1% lidocaine solution into subacromial space & repeat special impingement test - (+) = elimination or significant reduction of pain

Treatment

General Measures

- Pain reduction & avoidance of aggravating activity. PRICE or METH, NSAIDs. Ensure proper warm-up prior to activity

Massage Therapy - warm hydro if chronic, MLD and cold hydro if acute. Swedish, petrissage, stripping, GTO, PNF, jostling and shaking to related joint. Joint play to related joints. Frictions if chronic, followed with ice and stretch. IASTM, stretching in office (internal & external rotation; extension/flexion; add/abduction)

Osseous Mobes/Manipulation - address subluxations of AC & SC joints & cervical & thoracic spine. Direct GH mobes are indicated in cases that are not acute or hypermobile/unstable

Electrotherapy - TENS for pain reduction, Ultrasound therapy. Some studies show short term benefit with high-intensity laser therapy (HILT)

Acupuncture - Local shoulder point & LI4, 15, 16, SI3, 10, SJ5, 14

Medications - NSAIDs (short term), glyceryl trinitrate/nitroglycerin

Surgery (last resort) - depends on cause (open or arthroscopic)resection of distal clavicle, excision of osteophytes, repair rotator cuff tear, acromioplasty, subacromial decompression

Follow-up

Rehabilitation Program

- Ensure proper warm-up before activity. Acute goals - relieve pain & inflammation. Ice & rest shoulder, avoid aggravation. PFROM, pendulum arm swings, AROM, and stretching as tolerated (esp. posterior capsule)
- Subacute goals - normalize ROM, perform symptom free ADLs, ↑ strength & flexibility. Progress to PFAROM then mild resistance exercises (weights, tubing, aqua aerobics). Eventually progress to more advanced activities (increased resistance, activities that mimic sport or work activity, PNF)

Prevention/Patient Education - Evaluation of sport or work technique may be needed to observe ergonimics. Avoid sleeping on a hard mattress with shoulder abducted over head

Prognosis - Depends on coexisting factors (instability, arthritis, labral or cuff tears, longer standing condition in older patient). 60-90% of simple cases will usually resolve quickly to pre-injury status (2-6 wks). Complicated cases can take longer & may need secondary consultation.

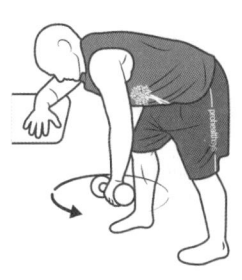

Swimmer

Assessment

prohealthsys

Basics

Definition: inability to maintain the humeral head centered in the glenoid fossa due to laxity of the shoulder capsule, ligaments &/or rotator cuff muscle imbalances or congenital joint anomalies

Degrees of instability

- **Apprehension** - fear shoulder will dislocate
- **Subluxation** - transient partial separation of articular surfaces - humeral head usually spontaneously returns to normal position
- **Dislocation** - complete articular separation

Types of glenohumeral instability - *Anterior inferior* (80% of cases) humeral head slides anterior & inferior. *Posterior* (~10%) humeral head slides posteriorly. *Multidirectional* (~10%)

Grades of instability

Grade	Description
WNL	0-25% translation
1	25-50% translation, humeral head riding up on glenoid labrum
2	50-75% translation, head rides up & over glenoid labrum, immediately reduces
3	> 75% translation & humeral head remains dislocated

Pathophysiology:

- *Traumatic:* instability secondary to damage of the rotator cuff, glenoid labrum &/or GH ligaments
  - *Direct trauma* - tackle from behind with shoulder in abduction & external rotation or long axis traction force applied to arm, americana or kimura (jujitsu/MMA)
  - *Overuse trauma* - repeated overhead activities (swimmers, racket sports, throwers)
  - Intentional subluxation or dislocation - patient can voluntarily demonstrate instability
- *Atraumatic:* congenital anomalies may have familial tendencies & are more likely bilateral
  - *Generalized joint laxity* - these patients have less cross-linked collagen fibers in their capsule = increase flexibility
  - *Glenoind dysplasia* - shallow glenoid fossa, anterior or posterior tilt of glenoid

Demographics

Incidence: ~2-3% of population

Age: 15-30 (young athletes) *Gender:* ♀ > ♂ (2:1)

Genetics: specifics unknown but can be familial

Risk factors: **prior injury or dislocation**, rotator cuff damage, throwing, anatomical variation

Diagnosis

History

- General shoulder pain, worse with activity or certain arm positions (overhead activity, carrying objects at side, overuse, prior injury, throwing). Pain is better with rest or heat.
- Patient may note a **history of catching or locking** with motion or prior athletic injury (dislocation). Often associated with impingement symptoms (painful arc of motion)

Physical

Inspection: possible **sulcus sign** or redness

Palpation: possible **tenderness over joint** if it is inflamed or there are damaged fibers present. Trigger points & myospasm of rotator cuff

Motion: AROM & PROM may show **repeatable clunk or apprehension** with abduction & external rotation. **Pain/impingement with 80-120° shoulder abduction & altered scapulohumeral rhythm.** RROM - usually WNL (may be weak due to pain or coexisting damage)

Neurovascular screen: WNL - check axillary & suprascapular nerve function and radial pulse

Differential Diagnosis

- Glenoid labral tear or GH osteoarthritis, Biceps tendinopathy, Rotator cuff tendinopathy or strain, Shoulder impingement, Subacromial bursitis
- Any of above may co-exist with GH instability

Special Test (see yellow physical assessment text)

- (+) Load & shift (anterior & posterior instability)

Inferior instability tests

- (+) Sulcus test (arm dependant & pull down)
- (+) Faegan's test (arm abducted 90°)

Anterior instability (best done supine)

- (+) Anterior apprehension test, (+) Relocation test
- (+) Release maneuver

Posterior instability tests

- (+) Sitting & supine posterior apprehension test
- (+) Norwood's posterior drawer test

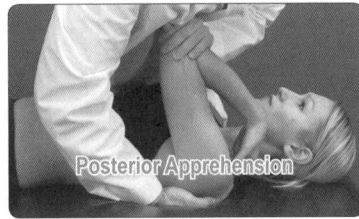

Posterior Apprehension

Diagnostic Imaging

- *Ultrasonography:* useful first imaging modality may detect full thickness tears
- *X-ray:* may show increased joint space, shallow glenoid & is useful to rule out other pathologies
- *MRI:* excellent for visualization of shoulder soft tissues & general bone detail; visualize rotator cuff tears & ligament damage - better seen with injection of contrast dye
- *Arthroscopic:* excellent for GH visualization

Treatment

General Measures - pain & inflammation control (PRICE or METH). If dislocated, refer for reduction ASAP. Consider short-term use of an arm sling. **Early PFROM results in better outcomes**

Massage Therapy - focus on shoulders & cervcal-thoracic regions. Swedish, MFTP therapy, myofascial release. Treat contralateral side first.

Osseous Mobes/Manipulation - shoulder manip./mobilization is contraindicated. Focus on area of compensation (scapulocostal, thoracic & cervical spine subluxations)

Medications - prolotherapy - tighten ligaments (capsular growth), NSAIDs, hydrocodone

Surgery - indicated if failure of conservative care. Open or arthroscopic surgery to reattach torn labrum or arthroscopic thermal denaturation of GH capsule (tightens up ligaments)

Follow-up

Rehabilitation Program

- Relative Rest. Start with basic PFROM as tolerated by patient. Ensure a good warm-up prior to activity. Progress to mild resistive exercises (gentle PNF, tubing exercises, water exercises, mild weight resistance)
- **Rotator cuff muscles provide a full 50% of the GH stability - strengthening & proprioceptive retraining of these muscles are fundamental!**

Patient Monitoring

- When determining a patient's return to competitive sports or physically demanding job
  - Normal scapulohumeral rhythm
  - Full AROM & PROM
  - Rotator cuff strength at 90% of opposite side
  - Pain-free activities of daily living (ADLs)

Prevention/Patient Education

- Educate patient on activities to avoid or how to modify ADLs to prevent injury

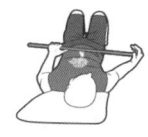

Prognosis

- Most respond extremely well to conservative care without dislocation or the need for surgery. In severe cases instability may lead to GH degeneration or progress to a full dislocation. The younger a patient the more likely a dislocation will re-occur (recurrence rate is ~90% if initial dislocation occurs in teen years, but only 15% after the age of 40)

Medical Legal - in acute trauma rule out fractures, neurologic, vascular damage & rotator cuff tears

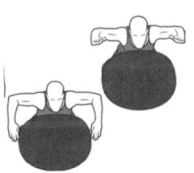

Assessment

prohealthsys

Basics

Definition: lateral elbow pain secondary to tendinosus & periostitis (most common condition affecting the elbow). **Synonyms:** tennis elbow, lateral epicondylosis, lateral epicondylagia

Pathophysiology: most often results from overuse injuries that damage the **common extensor tendon & extensor carpi radialis brevis**; inflammation leads to microtears of tendon & subsequent fibrosis (less commonly may affect extensor carpi radialis longus (ECRL), extensor digitorum (ED), or extensor carpi ulnaris)

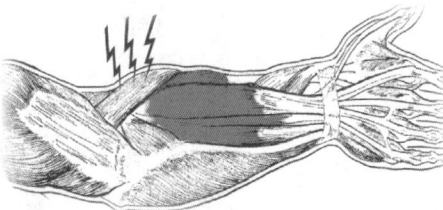

Demographics

Incidence: very common

Age: usually 20-40 yrs   *Gender:* male = female

Risk factors: repetitive microtrauma/overuse: wrist extension alternating supination & pronation, microtears in tendon

- **Systematic review identified 3 risk factors:**
  - **Handling tools heavier than 1 kg**
  - **Handling loads heavier than 20 kg at least 10 times per day**
  - **Repetitive movements more than 2 hrs/day**
- Tennis, typing, gardening (hedge trimmers). For tennis players: risk of overuse injury increased 2-3x with more than 2hrs of play per week & increase is 2-4x greater in players over age 40
- Video games, musical instruments
- Carpenters/plumbers/electricians (hammers)

Diagnosis

History

- **Lateral elbow pain** following activity without direct trauma to the elbow. Usually unilateral, gradual onset of pain. May have difficulty picking up items or weak grip strength (picking up book, griping steering wheel)

Physical

Inspection: usually WNL (no swelling or bruising)

Palpation: **localized tenderness to palpation** just distal & anterior to lateral epicondyle (origin of ECRB)

Motion: elbow ROM is usually WNL. AROM & PROM: pain with wrist flexion (stretch of ECRB). RROM: increased pain with resisted wrist extension (action of ECRB) - 'Cozen's Test'

Neurovascular: decreased grip strength on dynamometer. Pulses are WNL. In chronic cases, be sure to fully assess shoulder (weakness or instability of scapular stabilizers may cause lateral epicondylitis secondary to compensatory overuse of wrist extensors)

Differential Diagnosis

- Elbow arthritis or fractures, Cervical radiculopathy pain referral, Rotator cuff conditions, Radial nerve compression at elbow, Fibromyalgia

Special Test (See yellow Physical Assessment Text)

- (+) Cozen's = Tennis Elbow Test - forearm extensor muscle test. (+) Mills - stretch test
- (+) Book test - have patient lift object while extending wrist
- (+) Middle finger extension test (muscle test of extensor digitorum); also resisted supination

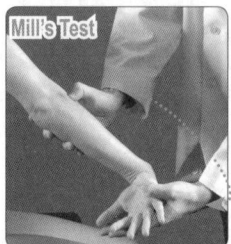

Mill's Test - examiner extends & pronates patient's elbow while flexing wrist & applies pressure over common extensor tendon

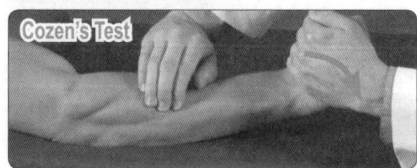

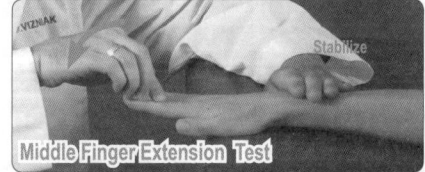

Diagnostic Imaging (usually not required) - May be useful to rule out other pathologies (MRI may show inflammation). Consider electrodiagnositcs for nerve pathologies

Treatment

General Measures

- *Acute:* relative rest, reduce pain & inflammation (PRICE/METH)

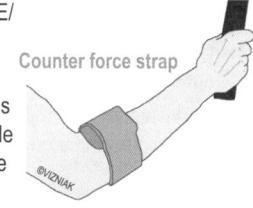

Counter force strap

- *Chronic:* counter-force brace or "tennis elbow strap" - provide compression, reduce strain

Massage Therapy

- ACUTE: MLD, diaphragmatic breathing. Compensations and unaffected side treated with swedish, petrissage, MFTP release, stripping, segmental petrissage in affected area (not on tendon). Vibrations on site, muslce compressions, squeezing, stroking distal to affected site. IASTM and gentle joint play

- CHRONIC: Diaphragmatic breathing, contrast hydro to flush edema, MFR release on restrictions, MFTP release, petrissage, ischemic compression on proximal limb. IASTM and frictions over tendon adhesions, apply a stretch while technique is performed if the adhesions are adhered to the sheath. Follow with stretch and ice. Joint play, PROM, passive stretches

Osseous Mobes/Manipulation - mobilization of shoulder, C-spine & T spine. Evaluate elbow join motions & correct biomechanical faults. One study showed that manipulation of wrist appeared to be more effective than ultrasound, friction massage, and muscle stretching/strengthening exercises for management of lateral epicondylitis (Struijs et. al. 2003)

Electrotherapy - therapeutic ultrasound over lateral epicondyle. Consider iontophoresis with NSAIDs has been shown to reduce pain. Low-level laser therapy 904 nm, total dose 0.5 to 7.2 joules

Acupuncture - local HT3, PC5, PC6, S13, S14, S17

Diet & Botanicals - increase water & protein intake, vit. A, C, E, tumeric (curcuma longa), garlic (allium sativum), ginger (zingiber officinalis), Boswell

Medications - NSAIDs (topical). Corticosteroid injection (controversial) - lateral epicondylitis is usually degenerative not inflammatory; steroid injection may inhibit collagen repair (do NOT inject into ECRB tendon)

Surgery (rarely required) - open release (Nirschl technique) of extensor aponeurosis - may result in lateral elbow instability

Follow-up

Rehabilitation Program - subacute stage: emphasize restoration of function of extensor muscle group. A progressive graded program can **improve flexibility, strength & endurance.** ROM for wrist flexion/extension & pronation/supination should be achieved prior to proceeding with a strengthening

- **Strength & grip training** should progress from isometric to concentric to eccentric contractions of the forearm muscles, especially wrist extensors. Finger flexion & extension, draw alphabet, squeeze ball, spread fingers against a thick rubber band

Prevention/Patient Education - job or sport modifications to improve ergonomics. Shock absorbing hammers, Proper arm placement, posture while typing, Tennis - improve back hand, talk to a professional about correct racket & technique

Prognosis - ~90-95% of patients with lateral epicondylitis responds to conservative care measures. Usually complete recovery occurs within 1-3 months. More rapid recovery with cervical manipulation & elbow physical therapy. Cases taking longer than 3 months should be referred for secondary evaluation

Assessment

Assessment

Basics

Definition: medial elbow pain secondary to tendinosus & periostitis. **Synonyms:** golfer's elbow, pitcher's elbow, or little league elbow in children & adolescents, medial epicondyle tendinopathy, medial elbow tendinopathy, medial epicondyle tendonitis, medial epidcondyle tendinosis (w/o inflammation)

Pathophysiology: repetitive use of flexor & pronator forearm muscles can cause micro-traumas inflammation, & possibly micro-tears, where common flexor tendon of forearm attaches resulting in disruption & degeneration of tendon's internal structure. Histologically, damage to involved tendons is described as angiofibroblastic hyperplasia tendinosis & fibrillary degeneration of collagen

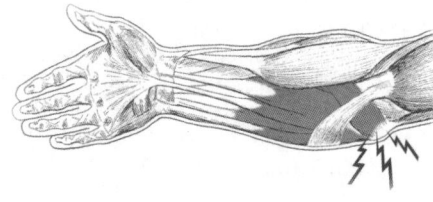

Demographics

Incidence: common (~1% of adults)

Age: usually 20-60 (but can occur at any age)

Gender: male > female (2:1)

Risk factors: repetitive work or sport activity

- Athletes who throw especially overhand (golf, baseball, racquet sports), factory workers, manual labourers, office workers
- Handling loads >5 kg (2x/min at minimum of 2 hrs/d), handling loads > 20 kg at least 10 x/d and high hand grip forces for > 1 hr/d
- Working with vibrating tools > 2 hrs/d

Diagnosis

History - Medial elbow pain following activity without direct trauma to the elbow. Pain is worse with wrist flexion, forearm pronation & gripping activities (see risk factors). Many patients (~40%) may have occasional &/or tingling sensation that radiates into their fourth & fifth fingers (suggests ulnar nerve involvement)

Physical

Inspection: usually WNL, look for signs of swelling, redness & warmth

Palpation: tenderness over medial epicondyle or common flexor tendon

Motion: AROM & PROM are usually WNL, possible pain with tendon stretch on PROM. RROM may show weakness or pain with resisted wrist flexion

Neurovascular: Decreased grip strength. Vascular screen should be WNL. Coexisting ulnar neuropathy may cause decreased sensation over medial hand/fingers, a positive Tinel sign

Differential Diagnosis

- Avulsion fracture, Arthritis, Ulnar collateral ligament injury, Cervical radiculopathy or Ulnar neuropathy, Osteochondritis, Thoracic outlet syn.

Special Test

- (+) Reverse Mill's test (flexor stress test)
- (+) Reverse Cozen's test (flexor muscle test)
- (+) Valgus stress test or moving valgus stress test
- (+) Grip strength weakness (dynamometer)

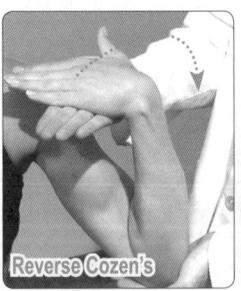

Reverse Cozen's

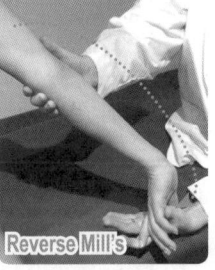

Reverse Mill's

Diagnostic Imaging

- *Ultrasonography:* shows excellent statistical reliability for the diagnosis of medial epicondylitis (Sensitivity: 95%, Specificity 92%, Positive predictive value 91%, negative predictive 96%)

- *X-ray:* to check for avulsion fracture, osteoarthritis, loose bodies
- *MRI:* may be useful to assess ulnar collateral ligament & ulnar nerve

Other - Consider nerve conduction velocity test if ulnar nerve involvement is suspected

Treatment

General Measures

- Relative rest. Remove cause (repetitive activity, faulty tool, poor ergonomic set-up). PRICE or METH as tolerated

Massage Therapy - see lateral epicondylitis.

Osseous Mobes/Manipulation - Mobilization of shoulder, C-spine & T-spine. Evaluate elbow joint motions & correct biomechanical faults

Electrotherapy - Microcurrent. Therapeutic ultrasound over medial epicondyle. Consider iontophoresis with NSAIDs has been shown to reduce pain. Low-level laser therapy 904 nm, total dose 0.5 to 7.2 joules - double blind clinical study on 324 patients: total relief of pain with consequently improved functional ability in 82% of acute and 66% of chronic cases (Simunovic 1998)

Acupuncture - local elbow points. Redness & swelling: SI6, SJ3, LV3. Inner elbow pain: LU5, LI8, LI12, SI1, SI11, **PC5**, PC7

Diet & Botanicals - increase water & protein intake, vit. A, C, E. Turmeric (*Curcuma longa*), garlic (*Allium sativum*), ginger (*Zingiber officinalis*). *Aloe vera* may help counteract wound healing suppression of cortisone (Pizzorno & Murray, 2006)

Medications - NSAIDs (topical). Corticosteroid injection (controversial) - only short term benefit, < 3 mo. (Stahl & Kaufman 1997)

Surgery (rarely required) - Open release & debridement of flexor aponeurosis - may result in medial elbow instability

Follow-up

Rehabilitation Program

- Subacute stage: emphasize restoration of function of flexor muscle group. After PFROM is established a progressive graded program can improve flexibility, strength & endurance
- ROM for wrist flexion/extension & pronation/supination should be achieved prior to a strengthening program. Strength & grip training should progress from isometric to concentric to eccentric contractions of the forearm muscles, especially wrist extensors
  - Finger flexion & extension
  - Draw alphabet, squeeze ball, spread fingers against a thick rubber band

Prevention/Patient Education

- Alter, reduce or remove repetitive strain activity. Review proper biomechanics, stretching, pain-free strengthening exercises

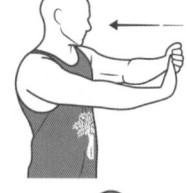

Prognosis

- ~90% of patients with medial epicondylitis respond to conservative care measures. Usually complete recovery occurs within 3 months. Predictors of poor outcome (Bot et al. 2005): Longer duration of complaint, musculoskeletal comorbidity, using "retreating" as coping style, less social support, using "worrying" as coping style

prohealthsys

Basics

Definition: compressive mononeuropathy (entrapment) of median nerve as it passes through the carpal tunnel (most common peripheral compressive neuropathy in body) **Pathophysiology:** increased pressure or irritation in the carpal tunnel causes median nerve compression and associated numbness, tingling, weakness & pain. Sensory fibers often are affected first, followed by motor fibers (autonomic fibers may also be affected)

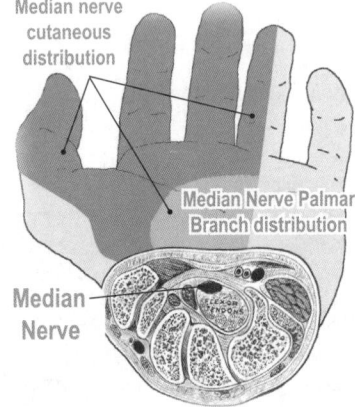

Median nerve cutaneous distribution

Median Nerve Palmar Branch distribution

Median Nerve

Demographics

Incidence: ~3% in general population, with ~10% lifetime risk of acquiring CTS = very common

Age: peak age 45-60 yrs (only 10% of cases occur in patients less than 31 yrs)

Gender: female > male (3-10:1)

Genetics: familial predisposition exists, related to multiple inherited characteristics

Risk factors: female, repetitive use (sport or occupational) - typing, construction, vibrating tools, massage therapist, dentist, chiropractors

- Decreased tunnel volume - subluxation of carpals, thickened flexor retinaculum, anatomical variation
- Obesity (increased BMI & low aerobic fitness)
- Diabetes, pregnancy, excess caffeine, nicotine
- B6 or B12 deficiency (controversial)
- Hypothyroidism (myxedema), RA, renal dialysis
- Trauma (fracture, laceration, dislocation)

Diagnosis

History - usually starts as **transient numbness & tingling over thumb, index & ring finger**, but usually NOT over palm of hand (the palmar branch of the median nerve does NOT usually pass through the carpal tunnel, leaving palmar sensation within normal limits)

- With changes in palmar sensation look for median nerve compression at pronator teres, brachial plexus (scalenes) and/or nerve root
- Hypothenar changes indicate ulnar nerve issues (ulnar canal, cubital tunnel, ulnar groove, brachial plexus, spinal nerve root)
- **Hand may "fall asleep," loss of grip strength or dropping objects (clumsiness)**. Symptoms are usually activity related - onset with driving, hand tool use, drawing, typing. Symptoms often wake patient up at night & may be relieved by shaking or flicking hand & wrist. Pain may radiate distally into hand or up forearm, elbow pain may be coexisting with medial epicondylitis. Some experience hand feeling abnormally cold, & may have a sensitivity to cold (autonomic fibers)

Physical

Inspection: possible swelling (compare bilaterally). Thenar eminence atrophy in advanced cases

Palpation: Local pain & tenderness over anterior wrist. Possible myospasm of forearm muscles

Motion: wrist motion is usually WNL. Possible decreased grip strength (dynamometer). Symptom exacerbation with wrist flexion

***Neurovascular:* very important!** Check sensation of median, ulnar & radial nerves. Decreased 2 point discrimination & light touch

Differential Diagnosis - Pronator teres syndrome, Ulnar or radial neuropathy, Raynaud's phenomenon, Cervical radiculopathy, Brachial plexus lesion or thoracic outlet syndrome, Trigger point referral pattern (pronator teres, flexor carpi radialis) may mimic carpal tunnel, Cervical spine subluxation, Transient cerebral ischemia

Special Tests

- **Best ortho test** is application of direct pressure over carpal tunnel with finger in combination with Phalen's for 20 seconds - should see exacerbation of symptoms (compression test)
- (+) Phalen's, reverse Phalen's test (60 seconds)
- (+) Tinel's, grip strength (dynamometer)

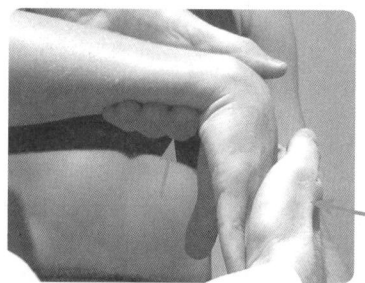

Imaging - may be warranted to rule out other pathologies or observe size of carpal tunnel & local edema. MRI is best for soft tissue evaluation

Other - electromyography (EMG) & nerve conductions studies (NCS), are considered the **'gold standard'** to confirm the diagnosis of CTS. Used to confirm diagnosis & determine degree of nerve compression with quantitative data

Treatment

General Measures - METH or PRICE, **relative rest** or change of activity, avoid aggravating activities & prolonged wrist positions. Wrist bracing or splints may be warranted - splinting wrist at night for a minimum of 3 weeks has been shown to improve healing time. Ice massage if acute, later switch to contrast or just heat as tolerated

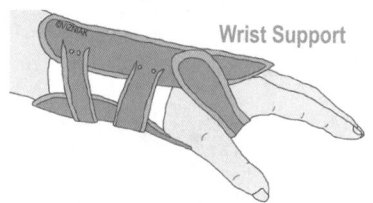

Wrist Support

Massage Therapy - treat both wrists (unaffected first). Circulatory work mixed in with trigger point release. MLD first, elevate limbs if edema is present.   Address shoulder SITS, then forearm with shearing, skin rolling, swedish on flexors/extensors. Frictions over flexor retinaculum, followed with ice and stretch (open and close hand

and ROM wrist). Joint play throughout. Finish with effleurage and cool wash with a cloth over affected area. Deep tissue massage in forearm flexors, scalenes & shoulder muscles. **IASTM** over the forearm & transverse carpal lig.

Osseous Mobes/Manipulation - do not aggravate patient symptoms. Distraction of the anterior wrist to stretch the transverse carpal ligament (flexor retinaculum). Carpal mobilizations. Anterior to posterior lunate mobe/manip. (avoid if A-P pressure aggravates). Address areas of potential involvement - C-spine, T-spine, shoulder & elbow

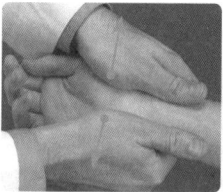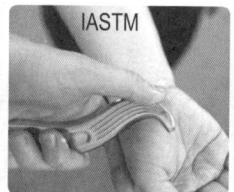

IASTM

Electrotherapy - ultrasound, phonophoresis, TENS

Acupuncture - local points, SP10, PC6,7, SJ5,6,10, LI4,5,9,11, SI4. Consider electro-acupuncture

Diet & Botanicals - B6 100mg/TID 2-3 months

Medications - short-term NSAIDs for pain reduction. Corticosteroid injection (controversial)

Surgery (rarely required & NOT guaranteed cure). May be indicated in chronic cases that show thenar atrophy, motor weakness & sensory loss. Surgical release (cutting) of flexor retinaculum. ~40% reoccurrence of symptoms in 5 years

Follow-up

Rehabilitation Program - alphabet exercise in cool water when acute. During day every hour for 1-5 minutes stretch neck, shoulder, wrist, hand, fingers. Later active grip exercises - tennis ball

Prevention/Patient Education - work-site ergonomic evaluation for stressors. Reduce BMI if obese & reduce intake of caffeine, alcohol

Prognosis - most mild to moderate cases respond well to mobilization & other conservative treatment. Older patients with more risk factors show a poorer prognosis. ~30% regardless of treatment (conservative or surgical) have reoccurrence within 5 years

Assessment

Basics

Definition: disruption of the ligamentous support between individual carpal bones &/or between the radius and the carpus resulting in a loss of structural integrity & associated biomechanical compromise of normal wrist function

Ligaments of the right wrist

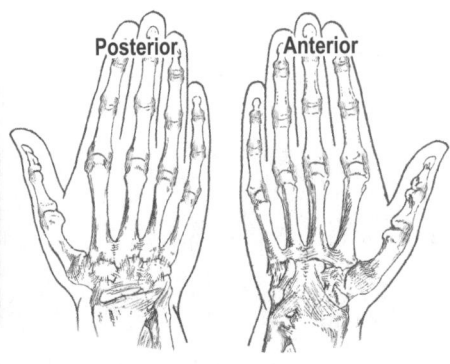

Posterior Anterior

Pathophysiology: realize that the carpals represent one of the most complicated regions of musculo-skeletal anatomy

Dynamic instability: bones may be in normal alignment at rest, but collapse under applied load

Static instability: occurs when enough restraints are lost that the bones assume abnormal alignment

Dorsal Intercalated Segmental Instability (DISI) - Scapholunate dissociation (most common)

Ventral Intercalated Segmental Instability (VISI) - Lunotriquetral dissociation

Carpal instability can cause other conditions (Carpal tunnel syndrome, Triangular fibrocartilage tear, Tendinopathy, Osteoarthritis)

Demographics

Incidence: more common in athletes & laborers

Age: adult (less frequent after age 50)

Gender: male > female due to risk factors

Risk factors: impact injuries, throwing, twisting, weight bearing, prior dislocations

Repetitive microtrauma, Degenerative joint disease (OA) , Rheumatoid arthritis

Diagnosis

History - Wrist pain following **prior microtrauma or single traumatic event**; fall on out stretched hand (specifically wrist extension with ulnar deviation). Median nerve compression symptoms (numbness & tingling in fingers) may be present with anterior carpal dislocations (lunate). Ask patient if they heard 'snap' or 'pop' at injury

Physical

Inspection: local swelling or bruising may be noted

- Possible visible protrusion or 'bump' of dislocated carpal my be visible

Palpation: **most diagnoses are achieved through direct palpation** of affected structures. Palpable tenderness & bony mass of dislocated bone (usually dorsal wrist). Anatomical snuff box tenderness is seen commonly with scaphoid fractures. Reactive myospasm & MFTPs of forearm & hand muscles may be noted

Motion: possible increased pain with wrist extension. **Crepitus or clicking with movement,** apprehension with radial & ulnar flexion. May observe or palpate repeatable crepitus with action

Neurovascular: usually WNL. With carpal tunnel compression numbness, & tingling may be noted

Differential Diagnosis - Hand or wrist fracture, RA, OA, Carpal tunnel syndrome, Triangular fibrocartilage tear, Ganglion cyst

Special Test (see Physical Assessment text)
- (+) Ballottement test (pain, increased ROM)
- (+) Bracelet test (compress patient's wrist)
- (+) Carpal joint play laxity or crepitis
- Grip strength weakness

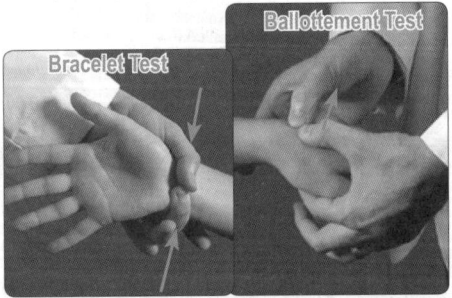

Bracelet Test

Ballottement Test

Diagnostic Imaging

- ultrasonography: may show dynamic instability with motion
- X-ray: standard views (PA, lateral, oblique), also include AP-clenched fist view or stress x-rays. Should not be more than 3 mm between carpals on AP. Terry Thomas Sign (> 3 mm gap)
- MRI may be of some use (usually not necessary) to show soft tissue damage & inflammation

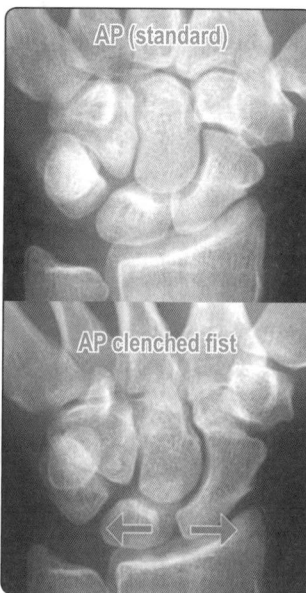

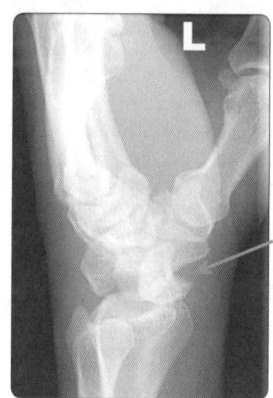

Lateral view - Lunate dislocation
(see arrow - 'spilled-teacup sign')

Laboratory - May be useful to help rule out other pathologies Rheumatoid arthritis (RA)

Treatment

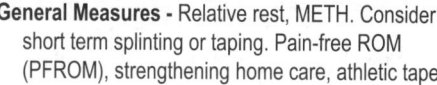
General Measures - Relative rest, METH. Consider short term splinting or taping. Pain-free ROM (PFROM), strengthening home care, athletic tape

Massage Therapy - Not directly over tissue during acute flare-up. Swedish, MFR, relaxation & massage of wrist & forearm. Consider cross friction massage and IASTM in mild cases

Osseous Mobes/Manipulation - Gentle mobilization may help reposition bones. Some clinicians suggest attempted repositioning after a trail of immobilization may be a better alternative than surgical intervention

Electrotherapy - ultrasound in an ice bath or cool water. TENS for pain reduction

Acupuncture - Local points PC6, LI4, LI11

Medications - consider prolotherapy to improve ligamentous healing & cause contracture of wrist joint laxity. NSAIDs for pain reduction

Surgery - indicated in chronic/severe cases. Many methods depending on specific instability - there are some new techniques involving bone-ligament-bone autograft from plantar plate of toes to reconstruct scapholunate interossues ligament

Follow-up

Rehabilitation Program - As sign/symptoms subside, progress to pain-free exercises. Increase ROM & strength. Hand & wrist conditioning exercises

Prevention/Patient Education - Educate patient on proper biomechanics & ergonomics

Prognosis - Minor instability usually responds well to conservative treatment. If untreated, may lead to chronic instabilities

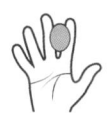   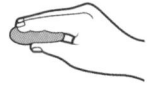

Assessment

Basics

Definition: stretching or tearing of the ligaments around the wrist. **Pathophysiology:** excessive ligamentous loading is usually secondary to hyperextension of the wrist following a fall on out-stretched hand (FOOSH)

- Can be due to a single traumatic event or repetitive microtrauma/overuse
- Unrecognized or untreated ligament injuries may result in wrist instability which leads to progressive degeneration & loss of function
- Wrist sprains occur in conjunction with:
  - Carpal fractures (scaphoid most commonly)
  - Carpal dislocation (lunate most common)
  - Triangular fibrocartilage tear

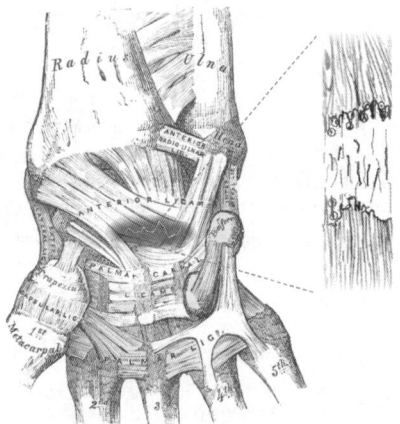

Demographics

Incidence: 2.5% of US ER visits are for wrist sprain

Age: 15-35 peak (may occur at any age)

Gender: male > female (more physical lifestyles)

Risk factors:

- Fall on out-stretched hand (FOOSH) - common
- Laborers involved in activities that require lots of hand & wrist use (massage therapists, physiotherapists, construction workers, factory workers, office workers)
- Athletes (gymnastics, golfers, skiers, bowlers, hockey, football, rock climbers)
- Students learning osseous manipulation (chiropractic, naturopathic, medical, physio)

Diagnosis

History

- **Pain localized to the wrist**, usually dull ache but sharp when challenged with ROM or palpation. **Prior trauma** (either single event or repetitive) - exact mechanism is important to give clues to specific tissue injury. Patient may have heard a 'pop' at time of injury
- Swelling is common (compare to unaffected wrist). Patient is usually unable to perform certain wrist & hand ADLs due to pain (open door or jar). Look for history of prior wrist injuries

Physical

Inspection: possible swelling (may be subtle). Usually no or mild bruising (with bruising suspect fracture)

Palpation: **local tenderness with palpation.** Point tenderness in anatomical snuff box may indicate scaphoid fracture

Motion: Joint play of carpals may show local pain. Possible crepitus with motion. AROM & PROM are usually limited & painful in directions that challenge damaged ligaments. RROM may show decreased strength due to pain (dynamometer will show reduced grip strength)

Neurovascular: should be WNL. Careful exam must be done to rule out other coexisting injuries (nerve damage)

Differential Diagnosis

- Fracture of carpals (scaphoid), radius or ulna; Carpal instability, Carpal tunnel syndrome, De Quervain's tenosynovitis, Ganglion cyst, Kienböck disease, Avascular necrosis, Nerve entrapment (median or ulnar), RA

Special Tests

- (+) Ballottement test (pain, increased ROM)
- (+) Watson's test (scaphoid shift test)
- (+) Bracelet test (compress patient's wrist)
- (+) Carpal joint play laxity or crepitis
- Grip strength weakness

Diagnostic Imaging

- **Indicated in moderate to severe injuries** or if there is a failure to see improvement in first 2 weeks - suspect a fracture until 100% ruled out
- Ultrasonography - may show swelling or abnormal motion
- X-ray - useful to help rule out more visible fractures (avulsion, radius, ulna). Consider AP-clenched fist or stress view - should not be more than 3 mm between carpals on AP. Second series of x-ray performed in 2 wks to rule out occult scaphoid fracture
- MRI may be useful (usually not necessary) to show soft tissue damage & inflammation

Treatment

General Measures - conservative management for grade I & II. METH, consider short term NSAID use, brace or elastic bandage or taping

Massage Therapy

- ACUTE: PRICE, proximal MLD, Proximal limb: effleurage, palmar kneading, PROM. Distal; light stroking & muscle squeezing
- SUBACUTE: as above, METH, muscle stripping on MFTP that refer to injury site, grade 1-2 mobes, onsite longitudinal muscle stripping followed by short cross fiber strokes (late stage)
- CHRONIC: METH, MFR cross fiber frictions & IASTM, gentle joint play & ice

Osseous Mobes/Manipulation - address biomechanical dysfunction in wrist, elbow, shoulder & spine - focus on increasing motion of hypomobile segments. Avoid direct wrist techniques when acute

Electrotherapy - Consider TENS for pain reduction. Ultrasound to increase local blood flow & healing (use indirect technique to avoid excess heat production over bone)

Acupuncture - Local, SI6, SJ3, SJ10, LV3, GB34

Medications - short-term NSAIDs. Prolotherapy may be beneficial in cases of chronic ligament laxity. Some chronic cases may benefit from corticosteroid injections (controversial)

Surgery (consultation for grade III injuries) - may be indicated for severe or chronic cases. Can involve ligament or tendon grafts from other body areas of body to improve strength. Rarely partial wrist fusion or pinning may be done

Follow-up

Rehabilitation Program - Main goal: improve conditioning & restore function. Consider short-term taping of wrist, thumb, fingers. Exercise & stretch to minimize the potential for longer term loss of wrist mobility. Stress ball & gripping exercises

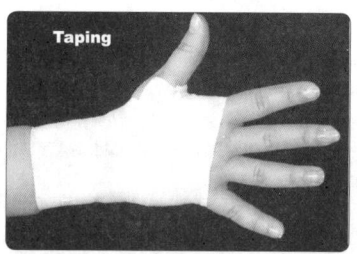

Taping

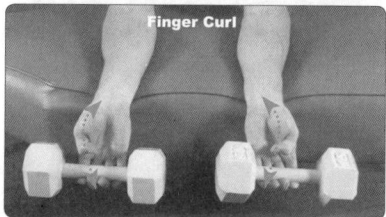

Finger Curl

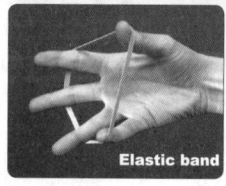

Elastic band

Racket ball

Prevention/Patient Education - educate patient on cause, proper biomechanics & appropriate warm-up. Educate on consequences of neglecting healthy behavioral & lifestyle patterns - arthritis & inability to work in one's chosen profession - (physio, chiros & massage therapists)

Prognosis - most patients with mild sprains can return to normal function in ~3-6 weeks following appropriate rehabilitation, moderate sprains may take 8-12 weeks. Risk of chronic recurrent issues if rehab. is not completed or return to activity too early. Severe sprain can be associated with cartilagenous injuries, instability & potentially future development of osteoarthritis

Assessment

Basics

Definition: fracture of scaphoid bone (scaphoid is also known as the navicular of the wrist)
- **most commonly fractured carpal bone**, accounting for ~85% of all carpal fractures.
Pathophysiology: usual mechanism is a fall on out-stretched hand (FOOSH) that results in loss of structural integrity of the scaphoid. Scaphoid is divided into 3 regions:

- **Proximal** which is the location for ~10% of fractures & has no blood vessels entering
- **Middle (waist)** which is the location of ~70% of fractures & has some blood supply
- **Distal** which accounts for ~20% of fractures & has the most blood supply
- Loss of blood flow to the proximal pole is noted in ~30% of fractures at the waist level & results in avascular necrosis (AVN) of the proximal pole of the scaphoid (the closer the fracture to the proximal pole the greater the risk of AVN. ~99% of proximal pole fractures result in avascular necrosis & displaced scaphoid fractures have a nonunion rate of ~60%

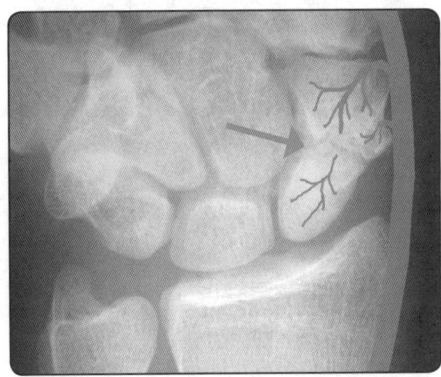

Scaphoid fracture (arrow) showing disruption of blood supply through waist

Demographics

Incidence: 1.21/1000 (relatively common) ~345,000 new scaphoid fractures per yr in US

Age: peak age 15-30 (can occur at any age)

Gender: males > females (2-3:1)

Risk factors: Fall (FOOSH), athletic injury (wrist hyperextension & radial deviation), motor vehicle accident

Diagnosis

History

- Wrist pain secondary to FOOSH, pain is worse with radial deviation & extension. Pain is better with rest & immobility. Patient will often experience grip weakness & difficulty with thumb movements

Physical

Inspection: possible mild to moderate swelling over anatomical snuff box

Palpation: **Pain with direct palpation of scaphoid** (90% sensitivity, 40% specificity) - other pathologies may also have pain with palpation (see DDx)

Motion: Possible mild decrease in wrist & thumb ROM, especially radial deviation &/or extension of wrist. Extension <50% compared with contralateral uninjured side is indicative of scaphoid fracture. Any motion that stresses damaged tissue, either through stretch or compression, may cause pain. Grip strength <10% compared with contralateral side indicates scaphoid fracture

Neurovascular: should be WNL. See pathophysiology for blood supply specifics

Differential Diagnosis - Other wrist fractures (radius, lunate, metacarpal), Lunate dislocation (may coexist), RA, sprain

Special Tests

- (+) Scaphoid fracture test (pressure in snuff box)
- (+) Bracelet test (compress around wrist)
- (+) Thumb grind test; (+) thumb abduction test

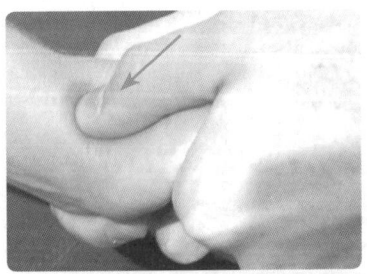

Scaphoid fracture test

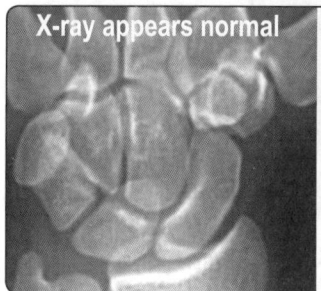
X-ray appears normal

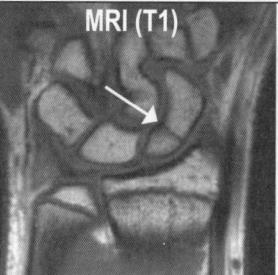
MRI (T1)

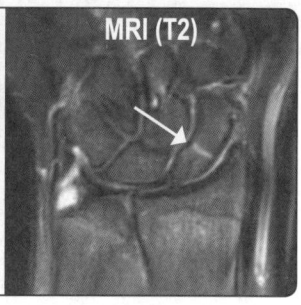
MRI (T2)

Diagnostic Imaging

- X-ray is usually the modality of choice to start investigation (PA, lateral, obliques & PA with ulnar deviation if not too painful). *Up to ~20% of scaphoid fractures are undetectable on initial x-ray*. If negative, consider re-xray in ~14 days as some fractures take time to show up

  - **With negative x-ray, misdiagnosis of a sprained wrist is common! - if in doubt try to have an MRI or CT done**

- **MRI is the gold standard imaging choice**, shows both osseous & soft tissue changes. MRI is **100% sensitive & 95-100% specific**. T1-images obtained in coronal plane are typically sufficient to visualize scaphoid fracture

- Consider CT or bone scan for diagnosis as well; CT is 94% sensitive & 100% specific for fracture

Treatment

General Measures - rest

- **Referral for surgical consultation** - early diagnosis of a scaphoid fracture is important because delayed diagnosis increases the likelihood of negative outcomes - avascular necrosis (AVN) or nonunion. Patients who are undertaking steroid therapy, who are pregnant, or who have systemic lupus erythematosus, haematological disorders or renal failure, are all at high-risk of developing AVN. Incidence of avascular necrosis has been estimated to be 2-9% of scaphoid fractures. If fracture is suspected consider firm brace or cast immobilization, there is a debate if casting or surgery offers a better outcome

Massage Therapy -

- Immobilized: MLD proximal to cast, effleurage, slow palmar kneading, mid range pain-free

PROM proximal and distal joints. Vibrations though cast. Light stroking, muscle squeezing, vibrations distal to cast (if possible?)

- Immobilization removed: contrast hydro or deep moist heat, MLD, Swedish, repetitive petrissage, ischemic compressions. Muscle squeezing to muscles suffering disuse atrophy. Pain-free mid-range PROM and joint play hypomobile joints. Skin rolling, spreading. Once pins/external fixation devices removed, treat scar formation.

Surgery - surgical stabilization is warranted with proximal scaphoid fractures (↓ blood supply)

Follow-up

Rehabilitation Program - after 3-6 weeks perform PFROM actions. Encourage elbow & shoulder ROM. After 6 weeks consider progressing to mild resistive exercises (water resistance in pool), eventually to grip strength exercises and ADLs

Prevention/Patient Education - Nonunion is ~20% more common in smokers - STOP smoking. Consider the use of a wrist brace when engaging in risky activities (skating, sports)

Prognosis - 90% of scaphoid fractures heal if treated early. Distal 1/3 scaphoid fractures takes ~4-8 weeks. Middle (waist) take 6-12 weeks to heal. Proximal scaphoid fracture takes 12-20 weeks & are more prone to non-union and AVN. With non-union or AVN there is increased risk of carpal instability, osteoarthritis & loss of function.

Medical Legal - ~ 40% of malpractice cases at the wrist relate to scaphoid fractures and/or perilunate dislocations - don't miss it & refer for secondary consultation if there is any doubt! If a scaphoid fracture is suggested, but not confirmed - treat it as a scaphoid fracture.

Basics

Definition: damage to the fibrocartilagenous disc & associated ligaments at the distal end of the ulna (triangular fibrocartilage - TFC). **Synonyms:** Triangular Fibrocartilage Complex (TFCC), carpal articular disc, discus articularis, triangular ligament, triangular meniscus

Pathophysiology: injury usually occurs secondary to a single direct trauma (FOOSH) or repetitive overuse resulting in degeneration. In most people degeneration of the TFC starts in age 30 & increases with age - by age 50 most people have signs of TFCC degeneration

- TFCC provides stability & flexibility to the wrist & is an important attachment point for the extensor carpi ulnaris muscle
- During axial forearm loading ~20% of force is transmitted through ulna, ~80% through radius
  - This percentage varies considerably with radius, ulnar length & radial/ulnar deviation
  - A radius that is 2.5 mm short following a fracture or growth arrest will result in ~40% more axial load through the ulna & predispose to an increased rate of TFCC degeneration

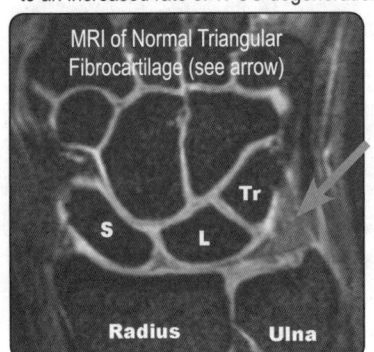

MRI of Normal Triangular Fibrocartilage (see arrow)

Tr
S
L
Radius   Ulna

Demographics

Incidence: unknown, *Age:* any, *Gender:* all

Genetics: congenital ulnar variation does predispose

Risk factors:

- **Traumatic injury** (Type 1): Falling onto out stretched hands (FOOSH), over supination/pronation with use of drill
- **Overuse/degenerative injury** (Type 2). Repetitive twisting or pulling movements of the wrist (gymnasts, working with heavy tools, carpenters, mechanics etc). Sports involving a racquet, club or bat

- Other risk factors: TFC tear incidence increase with age (TFCC degenerates with age). Ulna congenitally longer than radius (ulnar variance) increases risk. Previous history of distal radius or ulna fracture puts individuals at an increased risk of a degenerative tear (Type 2)

Diagnosis

History - ulnar side wrist pain worse with activity

- Type 1: fast onset - traumatic injury to wrist; either over-supination/pronation or FOOSH
- Type 2: slow onset - repetitive activities involving wrist (gymnastics or carpentry); patient may also report a previous wrist injury
- Patient may have weakness with rotational movements of the wrist or increased pain with compression. Painful click or snapping of wrist is common, better with rest, bracing or ice

Physical

Inspection: often WNL, swelling, abrasions, bruising if recent trauma

Palpation: **tenderness in dorsal depression distal to ulnar styloid,** around ulnar styloid or between triquetrum and ulnar styloid

Motion: pain with forced forearm pronation & supination. Pain with a clenched fist combined with ulnar deviation. Painful click may be noticed during wrist motions (also present in many other wrist conditions, such as carpal instability which may coexist!). RROM may show decreased grip strength due to pain. Rarely, subluxation of the extensor carpi ulnaris tendon may be observed

Neurovascular: WNL

Differential Diagnosis

- Fracture (carpal, ulnar styloid, metacarpal base), Carpal instability or dislocation, Ulnar nerve entrapment (Tunnel of Guyon), Extensor and flexor carpi ulnaris pathologies

Special Tests

- (+) TFCC Load test: ulnar deviation, axial compression & rotation or shearing of wrist
- (+) TFC dorsal glide test: examiner pushes

prohealthsys

pisiform/triquetrum posteriorly while stabilizing the ulna; pain/laxity may indicate a TFCC tear

- Press test: patient attempts to raise body off a chair while pushing on arm rests with both hands

Diagnostic Imaging

- X-ray is useful to rule out fractures, dislocations & to observe joint space (ulnar variance)
- Wrist Arthrography is rarely used (high incidence of false positive findings) - arthrography with multi detector computed tomography (MDCT) is 92-94% as accurate as arthroscopy for detecting TFCC tears (De Fillipo et al., 2010)
- Wrist Arthroscopy is considered the gold standard for TFCC tear diagnosis (invasive technique)
- **MRI provides up to 90% accuracy** for identifying TFCC tears (see image below)

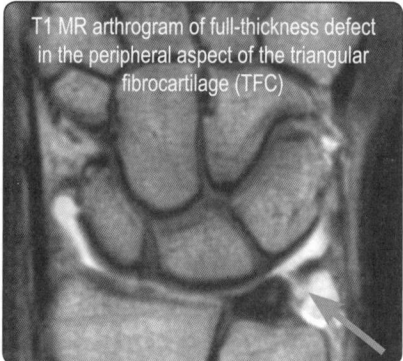

T1 MR arthrogram of full-thickness defect in the peripheral aspect of the triangular fibrocartilage (TFC)

Treatment

General Measures - relative rest. PRICE or METH with immobilization/bracing, K-tape, consider short-term NSAID use.

Massage Therapy

- ACUTE: PRICE or METH, MLD, diaphragmatic breathing. Compensations and unaffected side treated with swedish. MFTP release, muscle stripping, segmental petrissage in affected area (not on tendon). Vibrations on site. Muscle squeezing, stroking distal to affected site. Pain-free PROM on proximal and affected joints. Gentle joint play
- CHRONIC: METH, MFR, ischemic compression on proximal limb. Frictions or IASTM over TFCC, apply a stretch while technique is performed, Follow with stretch and ice.

- Trigger point therapy, MFR & IASTM may be useful for decreasing tension on the TFCC due to strain of connected muscles

Electrotherapy - Consider TENS for pain reduction. Microcurrent & ultrasound may promote healing

Acupuncture - local wrist points LU7-10, LI3-5, HT4-8, SI3-7, PC4-8, SJ3-9, GB34

Medications - NSAIDs, topical castor oil packs to promote healing & reduce pain/inflammation. Prolotherapy may help strengthen damaged ligaments around wrist & TFCC

Surgery - Arthroscopic surgery - useful for simple tears in the vascular, peripheral region of the TFCC. If the avascular disc has been torn, debridement is required. Open surgery - required for more complex tears of ligaments that require reattachment. Ulnar shortening - may be done for chronic injury or degenerative TFCC (Type 2); relieves pressure on the TFCC and tightens associated ligaments to increase stabilization

Follow-up

Rehabilitation Program - after relative immobilization & appropriate healing, progress to pain-free wrist ROM (pay particular attention to supination, pronation & ulnar deviation). Apply cold to wrist after activity, then eventually progress to wrist & grip strengthening exercises

Prevention/Patient Education - Avoid aggravating activities & re-injury - too early return to activity can lead to a chronic problem. Consider use of wrist brace during risky activities. Work modification or restriction may be required.

Prognosis - Most mild TFCC tears respond well to conservative care. Periphery of the TFCC has a good blood supply, tears in this region are usually self limiting; tears in the central avascular area have limited to no healing capacity & surgical intervention is required

- Arthroscopic debridement surgery has good to excellent results in ~85% of cases. ~60% of patients with positive ulnar variance will worsen over time & ulnar shortening may be required

Assessment

Basics

Definition: usually asymptomatic, fluid-filled, benign, lumps (cysts) that occur along joints or tendons of the wrist & hand most commonly (may occur in foot/ankle) **Synonyms:** ganglia, ganglion, hand cyst, hand tumor, wrist tumor, mucoid cyst, dorsal wrist ganglion, volar wrist ganglion, bible cyst

Pathophysiology: current research suggests hyaluronic acid eats away at the synovial capsular interface resulting in the pooling of mucin lakes composed of glucosamine, albumin, globulin & hyaluronic acid; as mucin pools a cysts formation is observed through the skin

- ~70% occur on the dorsal wrist & ~75% of dorsal wrist ganglions have an attachment (stalk) to the scapholunate ligament

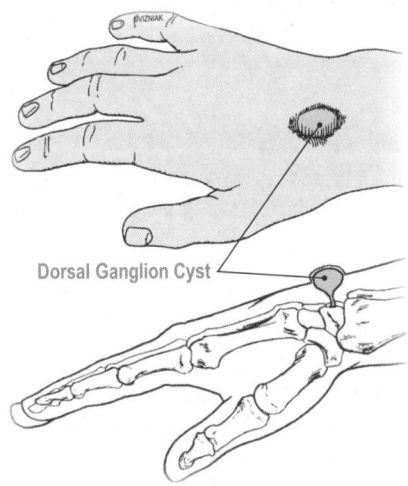

Dorsal Ganglion Cyst

Demographics

Incidence: very common

Age: peak age 20-30 yrs (can occur 15-90 yrs)

Gender: female > male (3:1)

Risk factors:

- Activities & jobs that cause repetitive or excessive wrist movements or place pressure over the hand & wrist (machine operators & hairdressers)
- Osteoarthritis & joint/tendon injury of hands & feet may increase risk
- Pre-existing anatomical defect may allow possible herniation of synovial sheath

Diagnosis

History

- Often **painless mass on wrist**, occasionally painful. Usually insidious onset however, some people report minor or major trauma prior to ganglion appearance
- If painful, it is usually transient pain that comes & goes (rarely chronic). May limit ROM or have affect on ADLs (decreased grip strength). If painful may be worse with excessive wrist use & better with rest. Rarely cyst may cause impingement or compress neurologic structures & cause numbness tingling & weakness

Physical

Inspection: **visible mass on dorsal or ventral wrist** (not always visible)

Palpation: often tender mass ranging in consistency from soft to rigid, over wrist joint or tendon sheath. Cyst is attached to deep tissue (not skin) & should not move around with skin & superficial fascia. Joint cysts are usually larger & soft; tendon cysts are often smaller & hard

Motion: depending on location, may limit full AROM or PROM. Grip strength may be weak due to pain

Neurovascular: WNL, unless cystic mass compressing vessels or nerves

Differential Diagnosis

- Infection (red, swollen, painful), Tenosynovitis, Sarcoma (very rare), Lunate or other carpal dislocation, Lipoma, Rheumatoid or Osteoarthritis

Special Test

- **Finger extension test** may be useful in diagnosis of occult wrist ganglia (92% diagnostic accuracy)
- Allen test – pre-surgery used to test for radial artery occlusion by anterior ganglion cysts

Diagnostic Imaging

- Consider MRI or ultrasonography to confirm diagnosis
- Ultrasonography - quick & inexpensive - sed to evaluate nature of cyst (fluid-filled or solid) & to

see if an artery or blood vessel is contributing to the existence of the cyst

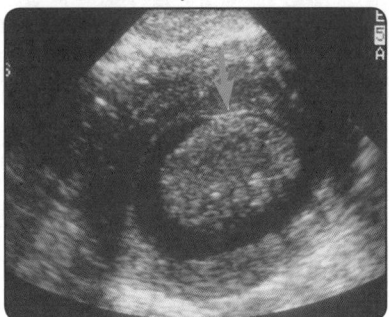

Ultrasonography of Ganglion Cyst

- MRI - excellent for soft tissue visualization
- X-ray - may be useful to observe osseous changes & rule out other pathologies
- Bone scan may be used to look for increased local bone metabolic activity

Laboratory - aspiration of a ganglion cyst may be performed for fluid analysis to rule out infection. Cyst fluid typically contains glucosamine, albumin, globulin & hyaluronic acid

Treatment

General Measures - youtube: vizniak ganglion

- **No treatment is required**, unless there is pain, numbness or physical impairment. PRICE or METH. Not recommended: using a heavy object (bible) to strike wrist & rupture cyst - high recurrence rate (22-66%) & possibly even wrist fracture

Massage Therapy

- Local massage may be contraindicated due to pain with pressure. Relaxation, Swedish around the area of cyst. MFR may help decrease fascial pull on the cyst. Focus treatment of forearm/wrist flexors & extensor muscles, MFR, IASTM, trigger point therapy, pin and stretch.

Acupuncture

- 'Surround the dragon' - general technique for injured area with associated pain & swelling

Aspiration - placing a needle into cyst and removing the fluid, ~50% success rate. Consider aspiration followed by prolotherapy injection to cause inflammatory contracture of soft tissue to disolve the cyst

Surgery - surgery is a last resort for the condition, & is usually only considered if other treatments that are non-invasive fail to work after 6 months to a year, or if the cyst is impairing activity

- Fluid aspiration to drain cyst using a large-gauge needle, followed by injection with a corticosteroid which shrinks or dissolves cyst. Another variation, inject the area with a local anesthetic & make multiple punctures with a needle. Increase success rate to 40%, splint for ~2 weeks following aspiration/puncture. Increase success rate to 80% repeat 3 times

- Open or arthroscopic resection. Arthroscopic allows surgeon to inspect joint for underlying abnormalities prior to excising ganglion & results in a smaller scar. Both have recurrence rate of ~15%. ~4% recurrence when a small part of joint capsule is removed with cyst.

Follow-up

Rehabilitation Program

- Following surgery splint wrist for ~14 days. Start with PFROM eventually progressing to full return to activity

Prevention/Patient Education

- Given idiopathic etiology not much can be done for prevention. Patients should be advised against self treatments like crushing their ganglion with a book ("bible therapy"), as this may cause further injury and won't prevent it from recurring

Prognosis

- Usually good prognosis, recurrence is relatively common. In rare cases of cyst malignancy, prognosis depends on what type of cancer it is and whether it has spread

Assessment

There **is poor correlation between imaging results and symptoms** in most cases.[1] The American College of Physicians and the American Pain Society **stress the use of a detailed history and physical exam.**[3]

Only order diagnostic imaging only if it is VERY likely that information will lead to a change in treatment or diagnosis.

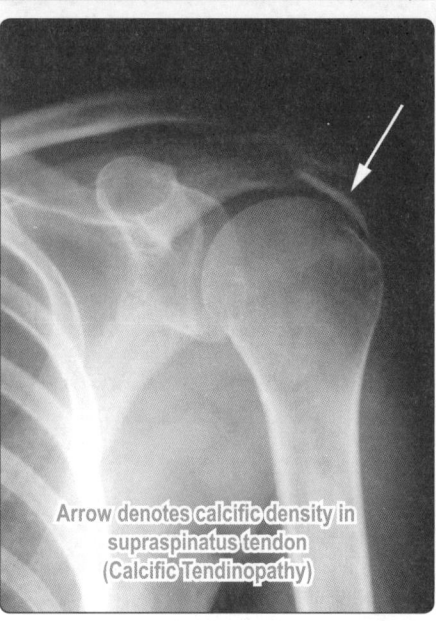

Arrow denotes calcific density in supraspinatus tendon (Calcific Tendinopathy)

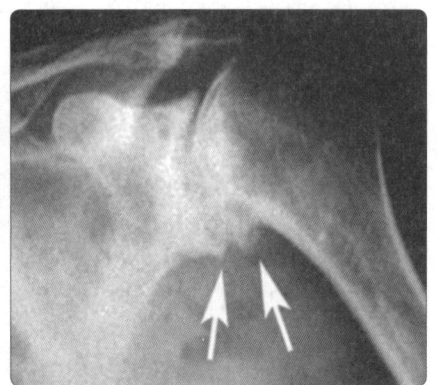

Findings DO NOT = pain

Fracture Screen

Fractures must be ruled out prior to out patient clinical treatment. (there are documented malpractice cases of clinicians mobilizing & manipulating fractures - you can be tricked...). Below is a list of commonly performed fracture screen tests based around the Canadian C-spine rules and general practice experience, more positive criteria increase the likelihood of fracture - remember **scans are NOT 100% diagnostic!** - For example, in scaphoid fractures there will be fractures present that do NOT show up on xray ~20% of the time (which are later confirmed in MRI) - **Treat the patient NOT their pictures.**

- *Four step* test (4 steps without pain or altered gait?) - **this test is still valid for upper extremity and spinal injuries** (observe for abnormal arm swing, rigid spine and very soft foot strike with each step)

- History of significant *trauma*? (FOOSH, fall from height, ballistic impact with force)

- **Older than 55?** (with age bones become less flexible & soft tissues are more fibrous)

- **Dark black bruising?** (rapid onset bruising indicates vascular rupture)

- *Resisted* isometric contraction (activated muscles pull on periosteum and bone attachments - with fracture patient is unable to develop muscle tension due to pain - excellent way to assess without displacing fragments)

- *Percussion*, light palpation, **Pain with squeeze** of bone (yes you can gently squeeze fractured bones, or even flex bone as in a sternal compression test)

- 128 Hz tuning fork, ultrasound (many false negatives - higher reliability if acute)

- **Limited or inability to move damaged area?**

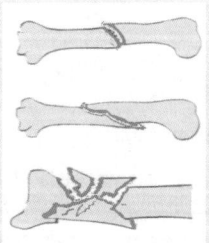

 youtube: **vizniak fracture screen**

WHEN A PATIENT GETS AN MRI FROM 10 DIFFERENT FACILITIES AND THE FINDINGS ARE ALL DIFFERENT...

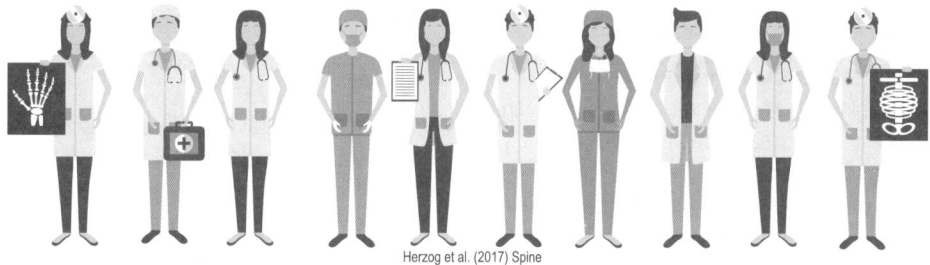

Herzog et al. (2017) Spine

Across all 10 study examinations:

- 49 distinct findings, 0 interpretive findings were reported in all 10 study examinations

- Only 1 finding reported in 9/10 reports

- Of the interpretive findings, 32.7% appeared only once across all 10 reports

- **Poor overall agreement on interpretive findings. The miss rate of ~45%** (sensitivity = 56.4%±11.7)

Imaging reports are nothing more than a written description of a picture of the body. Ask 10 people verbally describe a picture and you will get very different results (herzog et al.).

Radiologist should not write reports without details of the history and examination.

There is a poor correlation between imaging findings and presentation.

Assessment

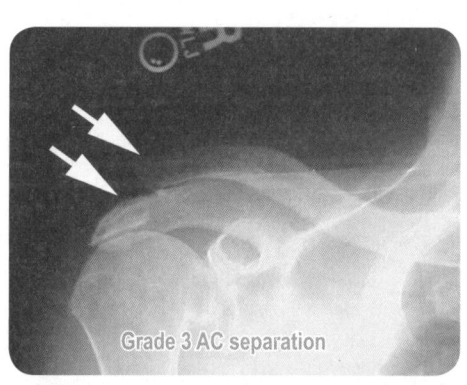

Grade 3 AC separation

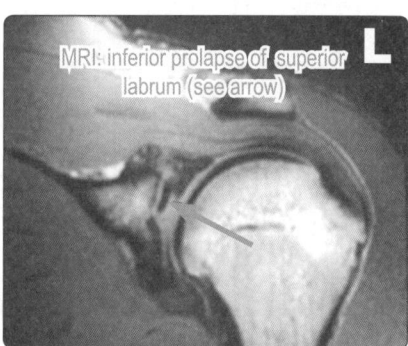

MRI: inferior prolapse of superior labrum (see arrow)

L

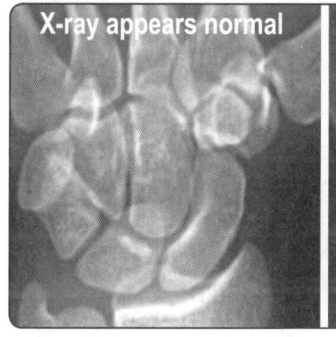

X-ray appears normal

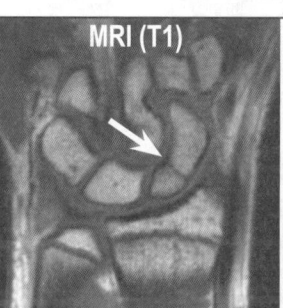

MRI (T1)

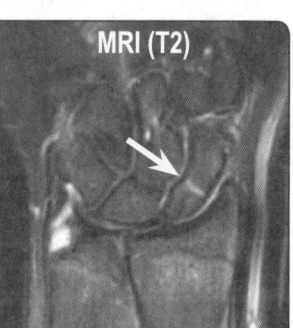

MRI (T2)

1. **Focus on Goals**

2. **Evaluate asymmetries** in posture and **imbalances** in movement patterns (right/ left, front/back, agonist/antagonist).

3. **Increase circulation** to the general area of pain or injury. This often means working with painful area indirectly by gently contracting or moving the surrounding muscles and soft tissues. The basic rule of the body is 'better blood supply = better healing'

4. **Increase strength and range of motion** gradually, over time. Release chronic muscle tightness (contract-relax-stretch is one of the best ways to do this). Evaluate contraction strength, look for action that are weak or cause shaking; work to develop **smooth controlled movements through the entire range**

5. **Restore symmetry and balance** (right to left; front to back, agonists and antagonists). Realize this process takes lots of time and often occurs through small incremental changes - cheer people on and let them know they are on the right track

6. **Dysfunctional movement patterns** need to be *reduced, modified* or *eliminated*. Identify activities of daily living that are impeded by pain and select movements that facilitate those actions (both physical and psychosocial)

7. **Be realistic** about your skills and knowledge when it comes to working with chronic pain. It is always better to refer to a qualified health professionals (doctor, chiropractor, physical therapist, acupuncturist, massage therapist or yoga therapist) than to make matters worse for them. Referral networks can be great for the business of better patient outcomes.

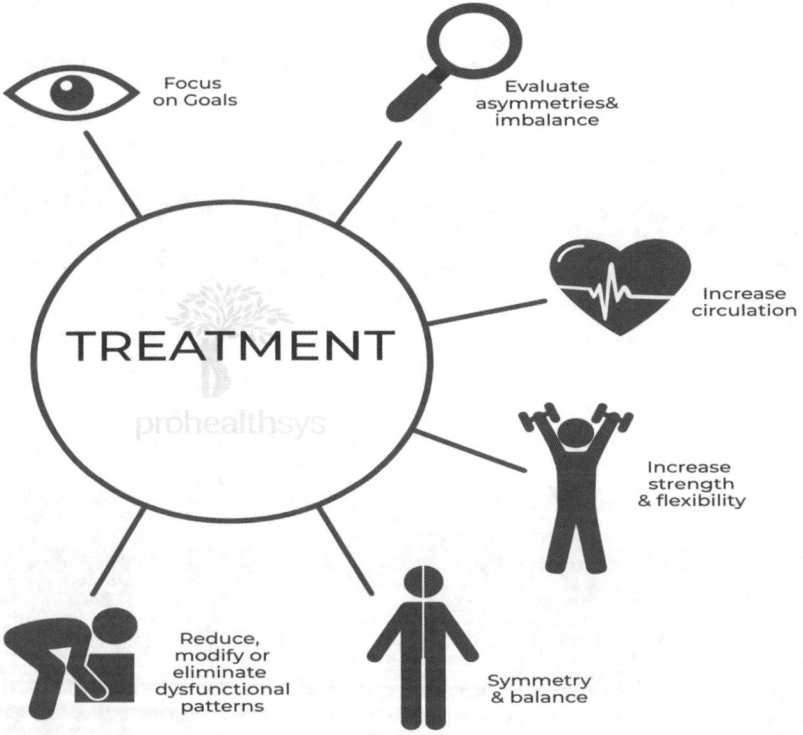

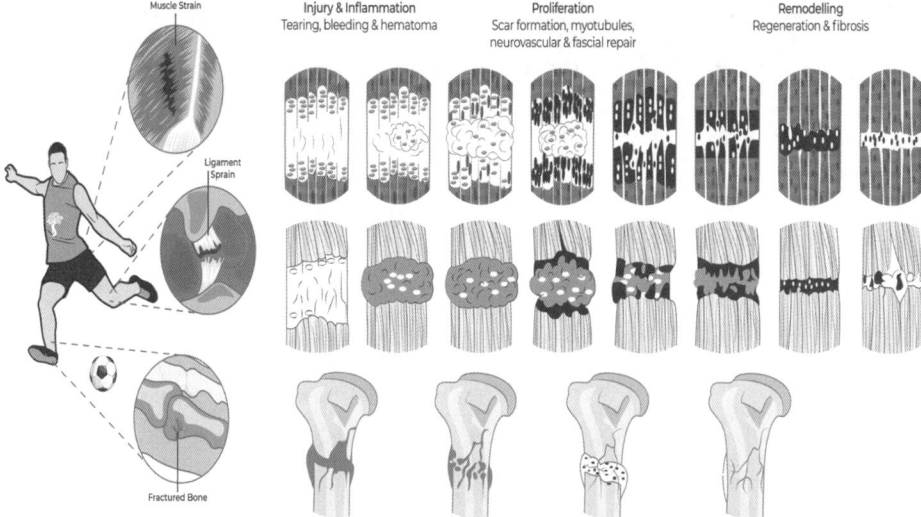

Muscle Strain

Ligament Sprain

Fractured Bone

Injury & Inflammation
Tearing, bleeding & hematoma

Proliferation
Scar formation, myotubules, neurovascular & fascial repair

Remodelling
Regeneration & fibrosis

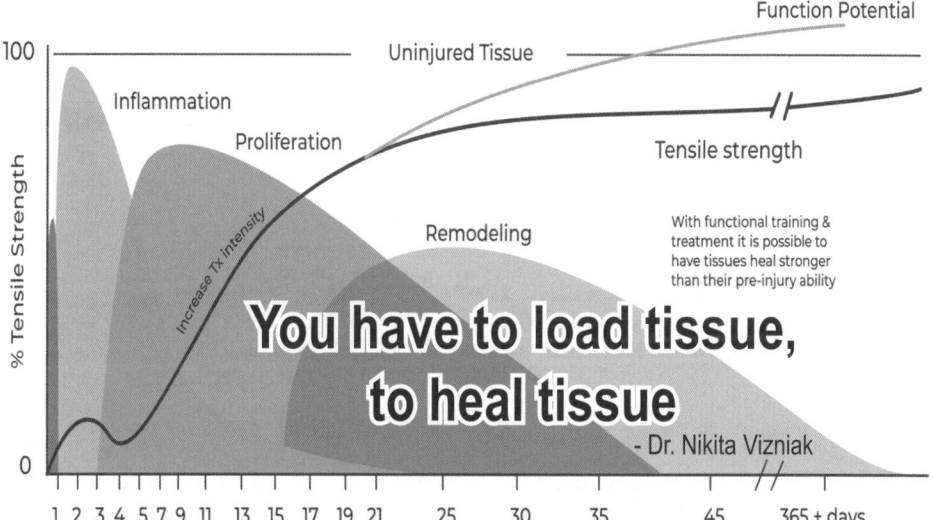

Function Potential

Uninjured Tissue

100

Inflammation

Proliferation

% Tensile Strength

Increase TX intensity

Remodeling

Tensile strength

With functional training & treatment it is possible to have tissues heal stronger than their pre-injury ability

You have to load tissue, to heal tissue
- Dr. Nikita Vizniak

0

1 2 3 4 5 7 9 11 13 15 17 19 21 25 30 35 45 365 + days

Actions

Pain is not always bad

Pain can tell us if what we are doing is causing body damage; however, you must remain active after a back injury even if it mildly hurts

Inactivity can lead to further tissue weakening and long term disability. Some tissue challenge & pain is necessary for proper, normal healing

Good Pain vs Bad Pain

'Pain should be respected, but challenged' Small pain is often OK. **If pain is >3/10, sharp or stops your breath then it is too much - look for joyful discomfort** ☺

Good pain you can purposefully control the intensity. Mild discomfort can lead to stronger muscles & more flexible joints

"Always laugh when you can, it is cheap medicine."
- George Gordon Byron

prohealthsys

The most powerful therapeutic option any clinician has is the ability to give their patient's the confidence to realize they can get better. A positive mind set & the belief of future wellness is the single most important factor in healing for most out-patient health care encounters.

Phase	~Time Course	Clinical Objective
1 Acute*	2-3 days (up to ~7 days)	• **Reduce pain; METH** (movement, exercise, traction, heat) • Emergency referral if required, prevent excess swelling/ischemia • Basic PFROM & activity as tolerated • **Address psychosocial concerns** (anxiety, depression)
2 Post Acute	2 days - 6 weeks	• Pain reduction, prevent early scar tissue adhesions • **Orienting repair tissue along line of tension** • Maintain normal muscle tone, ROM & functional capacity • Basic stretch, strength, IASTM, functional & proprioceptive retraining
3 Chronic*	3 weeks - 12 month or more	• **Neuromyofascial retraining functional capacity** • Proper alignment of repair collagen & myofascial tissue • Increase elasticity of scar tissue (increase ROM & strength) • Advanced stretch, IASTM, functional & proprioceptive retraining • Address psychosocial concerns (somatization, depression)

*Chronic recurrent episodes may be treated as acute during a flare-up; PFROM = Pain Free Range of Motion

Select Treatment Guidelines

Actions

Modality	Phase	~Duration	Modality	Phase	~Duration
Cold therapy			**Mechanical**		
Cryotherapy	1, 2	5-20 min	Bed Rest	1	0-2 days
Ice Massage	1, 2	2-5 min	Massage or IASTM	1, 2, 3	5-45 min
			Mobilization/manip.	1, 2, 3	1-20 min
Heat Superficial			Traction (in-office)	1, 2, 3	1-20 min
Infrared heat light	2, 3	10-20 min	Flexion-distraction	1, 2, 3	1-15 min
Hot packs	2, 3	10-20 min	Ext. compression	1, 2, 3	1-15 min
Paraffin	2, 3	7-10 dips (10 min)	**Exercise (in-office)**		
Hydrotherapy	2, 3	10-30 min	Passive	1, 2, 3	5-30 min
Laser	1, 2, 3	sec - minutes	Active (gym, yoga)	1, 2, 3	15-90 min
			ADLs	1, 2, 3	10-30 min
Heat Deep			PNF/CR	2, 3	5-10 min
Continuous US	2, 3	5-10 min	Bracing	1, 2	short duration
Pulsed US	2, 3	2-8 min	Work Hardening	3	2-8 hours
Diathermy	2, 3	5-30 min			
			Acupuncture/Prolo Dry needling/IMS	1, 2, 3	by technique
Electrical					
MENS (subsensory)	1, 2, 3	none established	**Nutrition/Herbal Medications**	1, 2, 3 1	entire treatment short duration
IFC (sensory)	1, 2, 3	10-30 min			
TENS	1, 2, 3	10-30 min			
Muscle stimulator	2, 3	10-30 min	**Surgery**	1, 3	emergency or last resort
Motor stimulation	2, 3	2-10 min			

Note: specific treatment régimes must be tailored to the individual patient presentation.
In most cases, medication use should be short term (long-term use can result in chemical dependency & mask important signs & symptoms). Surgical intervention should be offered only in emergency injuries or as a last resort when conservative treatments have failed (surgery is not a guaranteed cure).

Progress from least to most invasive with the Minimal Effective Dose

- Dr. Nikita Vizniak

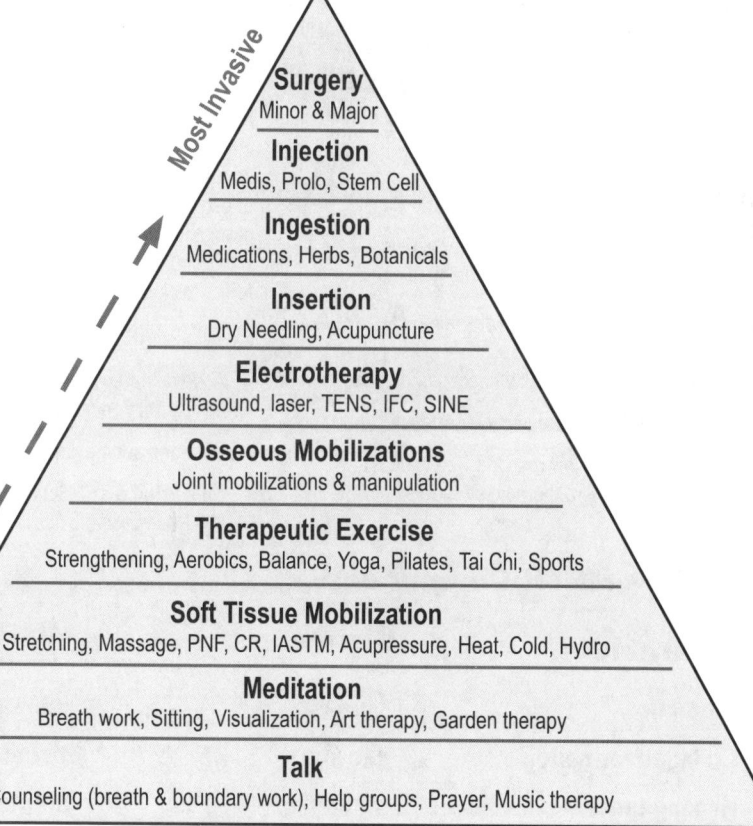

Most Invasive

Surgery
Minor & Major

Injection
Medis, Prolo, Stem Cell

Ingestion
Medications, Herbs, Botanicals

Insertion
Dry Needling, Acupuncture

Electrotherapy
Ultrasound, laser, TENS, IFC, SINE

Osseous Mobilizations
Joint mobilizations & manipulation

Therapeutic Exercise
Strengthening, Aerobics, Balance, Yoga, Pilates, Tai Chi, Sports

Soft Tissue Mobilization
Stretching, Massage, PNF, CR, IASTM, Acupressure, Heat, Cold, Hydro

Meditation
Breath work, Sitting, Visualization, Art therapy, Garden therapy

Talk
Counseling (breath & boundary work), Help groups, Prayer, Music therapy

Least Invasive

Actions

Nutrition/diet, activity and social support are the cornerstones of health.

This is not a complete list & individual practitioners may offer a variety of therapeutic interventions depending upon the local scope of practice & practitioner educational level, experience and preference.

US = ultrasound (therapeutic), TENS = transcutaneous electrical neuromuscular stimulation, MENS = microcurrent, IFC = interferrential current, CR = contract-relax, PNF = proprioceptive neuromuscular facilitation, IASTM = instrument-assisted soft tissue mobilization

Treatment plans must be specifically tailored for each individual patient; the **general rule is to follow the therapeutic order (least to most invasive)** with increasing levels of difficulty as tolerated by the patient. Numerous factors can influence progression through treatment (severity of injury, age, diet, aerobic fitness, general health, mind set to name a few). Phases overlap greatly & may relapse depending on patient healing ability, rest period & activity level. The number one factor in the development of a chronic injury is a return to full activity TOO HARD, TOO SOON!

Acute phase (~1-5 days)

- **Main goals:** relieve pain, prevent muscle atrophy without exacerbation, re-establish pain-free ROM & normalize biomechanical function - inflammation is a normal process in healing

- Low Pain motion is key - **the sooner you move the better the outcome will be**

Good Pain vs Bad Pain with Motion

Good pain challenges the tissue and you can breath through it ('joyful discomfort'). **Bad pain is sharp or stops your breath. Pain should be respected but challenged.**

METH (Move, Exercise, Traction, Heat)

- **Protect** - DO NOT re-injure damaged tissue (possible chronic condition & delayed healing)

- **Relative Rest** - short term cessation of use (1-2 days max) - continued excessive activity may cause further injury, delay healing & increase pain

- **METH** (contraindicated in compartment synd.)

  - Most patients will respond well to heat and movement as a therapy (see table below)

- Even with mild injury it is usually recommended that rehabilitation program is completed to avoid re-injury or development of a chronic condition

Post-acute phase (~2 days to 6 wks)

- **Main goals:** normalize ROM & biomechanics, perform symptom-free daily activities, & improve neuromuscular control & muscle strength

- **Warm up prior to activity;** key goal is restoring integrity & strength of dynamic & static stabilizers of region

- Isometrics progress to concentric exercises, then to eccentric exercises, & finally to activity/sport-specific exercises to potentially reverse degenerative changes. When performing strengthening exercises, it is safer to start out with low tension, followed by a gradual increase in force (avoids flare-ups)

- Tx includes AROM & mild strengthening activities

  - Aquatic therapy is helpful in encouraging activity with decreased weight bearing

  - Pain-free submaximal isometric exercises

  - Ultrasound & TENS may decrease pain; IASTM to promote tissue growth & healing

RICE vs METH Comparison

Parameter	RICE (rest, ice, compress, elevate)	METH (movement, exercise, traction, heat)
Blood flow	↓ Decreased	↑ Increased
Collagen formation	↓ Slowed	↑ Encouraged
Healing time	↑ Lengthened	↓ Shortened
Range of motion	↓ Decreased	↑ Increased

Psychology, nutrition & sleep (recovery) are critical to healing. Short term use of natural analgesics are of benefit - do not stop the natural inflammatory reactions that lead to healing (note corticosteroids can actually slow healing) - **Food is Medicine! Generally, treatments that increase local blood flow, neural stimulation & provide nutrient building blocks improve healing**

Actions

Remodeling phase (3 wks -12+ months)

- **Main goals:** maintain a high level of ability, prevent tissue contracture & reoccurrence of injury, maintain normal biomechanical function

- IASTM is one of the best ways to reduce scar tissue formation & promote healing

- Patient should be able to perform isometric exercises at 100% effort without pain

- Begin unilaterally with weights, using low weight & higher repetitions to monitor form & technique; slowly increase the weight as tolerated as long as pain/inflammation is not increased afterwards

- <u>**DO NOT**</u> increase weight or intensity too rapidly, may lead to a chronic injury (**10% per week max**)

- Once concentric strengthening is tolerated, patient may begin eccentric strengthening (puts most strain on muscle), supervised exercising & slow progression of weight is recommended

- If patient experiences pain or stiffness, then decrease weight or intensity to a tolerable level

- **When affected side is within 10% of unaffected side, consider advancing to a more challenging work or sport specific activities**

- **Warm up & post activity stretching are essential**; address other regions of compensation (posture, restriction, imbalance, ergonomics)

Functional stage (2 weeks to 6 months)

- Patient should have a normal gait pattern & can begin fast walking

  - When patient can ambulate for 20-30 minutes at fast speed without pain or stiffness, short periods of jogging can be added to fast walking

Elite athletes & the general population can use similar protocols. The higher the patient's ability prior to injury the faster they can progress through treatment and the faster the recovery.

DO NOT become a victim of pressure from coaches, parents or the patient themselves, maintain your professional demeanor & stick to your recommended treatment for the long-term benefit of the patient (athletes are more than their sport)

Be **SMART** when setting goals

- ☐ Specific
- ☐ Measurable
- ☐ Attainable
- ☐ Realistic
- ☐ Timed (completion date)

- During later stages, plyometric exercises may be used to increase speed & power during training

  - Low intensity exercises may be used initially (eg, jumping rope), followed by higher-level exercises as tolerated (eg, side jumping over a low object, jumping on & off a box)

- **Higher intensity exercises are associated with a higher rate of injury & should be performed with supervision**

- Isometric strength & flexibility testing should be done prior to return to ensure no subtle deficits are present that lead to recurrent or chronic injury

- Clinician must impress upon patient the importance of mild stretching & warm-up prior to activities to prevent re-injury

- In patients whose injury was due to poor biomechanics, address underlying causes

- Patient should be supervised during stretching & exercise in order to assess poor technique & correct it

- Conditioning & proper techniques are important for certain athletes due to improper biomechanics which may result in tissue fatigue & damage

- Flexibility & strengthening exercises continue after returning to activity/sport to prevent recurrence

- **The importance of mental training/toughness, self talk & visualization cannot be over stated**

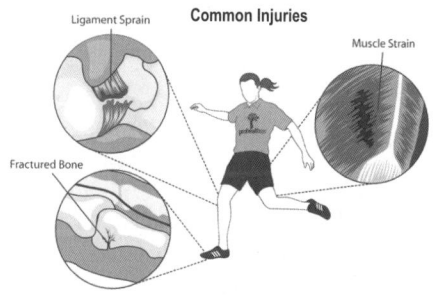

Common Injuries

Ligament Sprain

Muscle Strain

Fractured Bone

Actions

Shoulders should be relaxed, arms horizontally in front of you, and the mouse within easy reach

Keep your wrists straight and flat, NOT bent up or down

Your keyboard should be fairly flat, or on a negative slant

'B' on keyboard in-line with the center of your body

Use a light touch on the keys; try not to pound, even with a deadline just moments away

Keep your mouse as close to your keyboard as possible

prohealthsys

Poor

Optimal

90°-120°

90°-120°   prohealthsys   90°-120°

Shallow breath (poor oxygen supply)

Slouch posture (back pain)

Extended neck (stiffness & headaches)

Poor elbow & wrist angles (strain)

Too close to screen (eye strain)

No breaks or movement!

- **muscle weakness**
- **cancer risk**
- **back pain**
- **lower productivity & quality of life**

Shoulders back, down & relaxed - **easy breath**

Monitor at arms length

Eyes level just below top of screen

If possible tilt seat pan slightly forward (kneed below hips)

Feet on floor or foot rest (**take your shoes off**)

Sit back in chair for support

Neutral posture in all body regions

Take regular breaks, move often stand and walk!

Exercise is good for everyone. Thousands of studies and personal experience have shown the benefits. Exercise intensity should be modified on a specific case by case basis, but all age groups and physical abilities can benefit.

Contraindications to Exercise

1. Patient request to stop
2. Any chest pain that is increasing
3. Physical or verbal manifestations of shortness of breath or severe fatigue or wheezing
4. Leg cramps or intermittent claudication
5. Hypertensive response (SBP >260 mm Hg; DBP>115 mm Hg)
6. Pronounced ECG changes or cardiac arrhythmias (abnormal heart rhythms)

Exercise Benefits - Fast 14

1. Improves mood (feel better, ↑ confidence)
2. Increases lifespan
3. Maintains mobility & flexibility
4. Reduce body fat & weight control
5. ↑ memory, brain function & mental health
6. Increase coordination & muscle strength
7. Better sex life
8. Increase bone density (reduce osteoporosis)
9. Improves immune function
10. Increase cardiovascular function
11. Improves digestion & elimination
12. Lowers blood pressure
13. Reduces diabetes & cancer risk
14. Fundamental for all body healing

'Use it or lose it' is 100% accurate

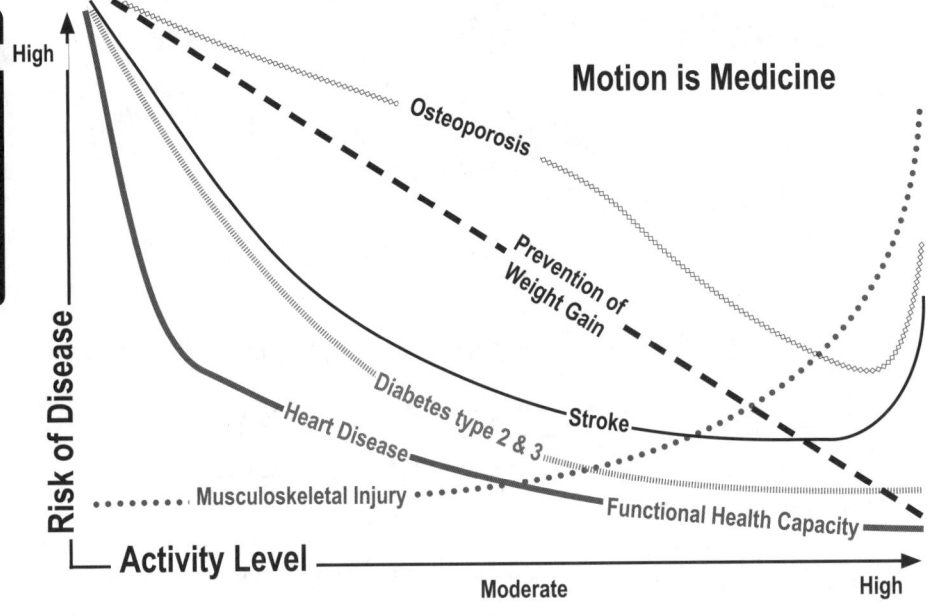

Motion is Medicine. For most conditions, activity reduces risk factors and improves functional health capacity. At extremes of activity, the risk of stroke, osteoporosis and musculoskeletal injury increases.
(Type 2 diabetes is insulin resistance associated with obesity, type 3 diabetes is Alzheimer's Disease)

"Those who do not find the time for exercise will have to find time for illness"
all good health care providers

Definitions

- **Rep (repetition)** = 1 complete movement (concentric & eccentric)

- **Set** = number of times a group of reps is done

- **1 RM** = 1 Repetition Maximum (the most weight that can be done for one rep)

- **Total volume** = reps x sets x weight

  - 3 sets of 10 reps with 100 lbs = 3,000

  - 10 sets of 3 reps with 100 lbs = 3,000.

  - Research suggests for hypertrophy **even though the number of sets and reps are different, the gains in muscle hypertrophy are very close to identical using the same total volume**

  - **For strength, studies show that the most important factor is the intensity.** The heavier you lift, the stronger you become.

Optimal Sets & Reps

Two meta-analyses measured differences in strength gains & muscle hypertrophy. comparing single vs multi set sessions. In both, **multiple set training came out on top. Eccentric contractions** (lowering phase) are ~10% stronger, thus increase total work volume

Can Training Reduce Your Injury Risk?

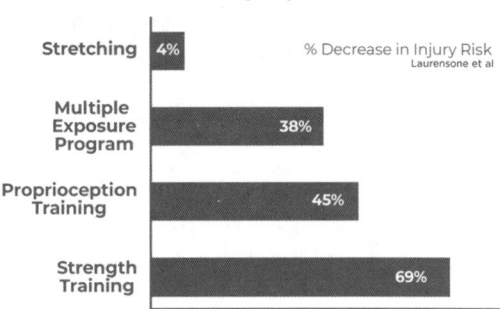

Train the motion, not the muscle

- Eccentric-focused sets ('*negatives*') can serve as a finishing set to slightly increase gains

- Lifting a slower eccentric phase, assures control of the weight down, keeping more tension in muscle-tendon units

- Generally a slower rep scheme is good for beginners to work on form and prevent injury

- **Studies consistently show greater total work volume = greater muscle growth**

Actions

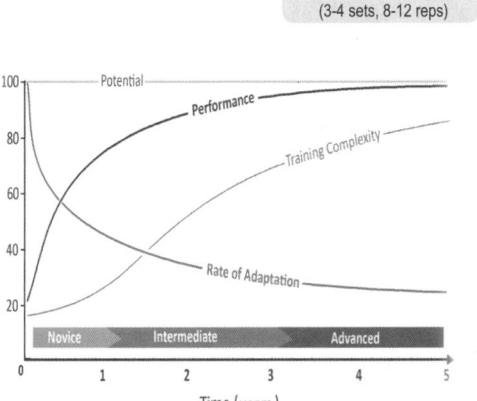

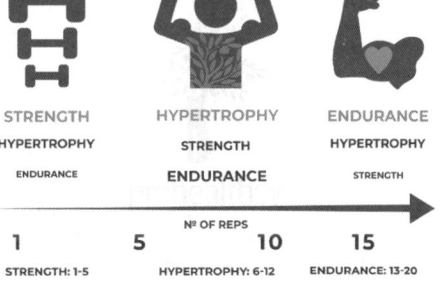

HOW MANY REPS
SHOULD YOU DO?

Resistance training is gradually & progressively overloading musculoskeletal system so it gets stronger. The research shows that regular resistance training will strengthen & tone muscles, increase bone mass, improve mental health and may reduce injury risk.

When muscles are stressed under heavier loads, they experience microscopic damage; in response, the injured cells release inflammatory molecules (cytokines) that activate injury repair. The greater the damage to the muscle tissue, the more your body will need to repair itself . The resulting cycle of damage and repair eventually makes muscles bigger and stronger as they adapt to progressively greater demands (see training effect).

Since our bodies have already adapted to most everyday activities, those generally don't produce enough stress to stimulate hypertrophy, and our cells need to be exposed to higher or different workloads. Atrophy occurs if you don't continuously expose muscles to some resistance.

In contrast, exposing the muscle to a high degree of tension, especially while the muscle is lengthening (eccentric contraction), generates effective conditions for new growth. However, muscles rely on more than just activity to grow. Without proper nutrition, hormones, and rest your body would never be able to repair damaged muscle fibers.

Adequate protein (amino acids) intake along with hormones, like insulin-like growth factor and testosterone, shift the body into an anabolic (growth) state. This repair process mainly occurs when we're resting, especially while sleeping. Repair is affected by rest, age, gender & genetics.

Sleep & Growth

Proper sleep is required for all aspects of health including muscle growth & healing. Lack of sleep can lead to:

- significantly slower reaction times on the psychomotor vigilance test; slower alertness means both lower mental and motor capacity
- increases error rate in tasks
- lower levels of testosterone and elevate levels of cortisol and other stress hormones
- when compared to people that slept 5.5 hours per night, people that slept 8 hours per night lost the same amount of weight, but they lost 55% more fat while preserving 60% more muscle. It's almost like sleeping your fat away

(Nedeltcheva, A.V., Kilkus, J.M., Imperial, J., Schoeller, D.A., and Penev, P.D. (2010)

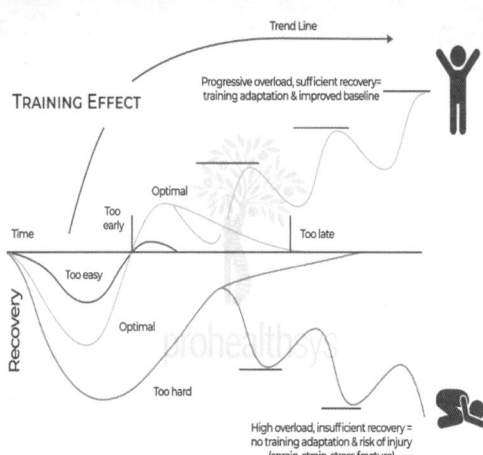

High overload, insufficient recovery = no training adaptation & risk of injury (sprain, strain, stress fracture)

Signs of Over Training

1. **Increased injury rate - greatest with:**
   - **Lack of warm up**
   - **Fatigue at end of activity**
   - **Full eccentric to concentric action**
2. **Persistent muscle soreness**
3. **Increased susceptibility to infections**
4. **Irritability, depression, insomnia**
5. **Loss of motivation, libido, menstruation**
6. **Halted progress (or regression)**
7. **Altered resting heart rate**

Timing on Exercise

- Most athletes notice the biggest performance changes within the first year of training, after that the rate of adaptation slows
- For muscle hypertrophy, studies tend to agree training at a moderate intensity between 60 – 75% of your one rep max, with roughly 4 sets of 8 – 12 reps of each muscle group, 2-3x/wk
- For muscle strength, training at a slightly high intensity of 80 – 90% of your one rep max with a range of 4 – 8 sets per muscle group 2x a week will suit the majority of the population and that's roughly 4x/wk week on a split.

(Peterson, M.D., Rhea, M.R., and Alvar, B.A. (2005) Applications of the dose-response for muscular strength development: a review of meta-analytic efficacy and reliability for designing training prescription. Journal of Strength and Conditioning Research. 19.4: 950 – 958.)

- Beginners and intermediate lifters also tend to be able to get away with higher frequency training while elite athletes or long-term lifters may benefit from more recovery.

Gauging Intensity using Heart Rate (HR)

The basic way to calculate maximum heart rate is to **subtract age from 220**.

220 - 40 yrs old = 180 beats/min max

- Moderate intensity: 50-70% max HR
- Vigorous intensity: 70-85% max HR

Remember train the motion not the muscle

Exercise prescription - get F I T T

Frequency: __ x/wk - find a balance between enough stress for tissue adaptation & allow enough rest to heal.

Intensity: effort during exercise (% of max). Balance intensity hard enough to overload the body but not so difficult that it results in overtraining, injury or burnout.

Time: how long each session should last. Varies based on the intensity and type.

Type: cardiovascular, strength and flexibility training. Based on goals & specific exercises performed

Cardiovascular training: 3-5x/wk, 60-85% 1 rep max, 20-60 min

Strength training: 2-3x/wk, 70-90% 1 rep max, 8-10 reps, 1-3 sets

Flexibility training: 2-3x/wk, 10-30 sec holds, 2-4 reps (yoga)

adapted from ACSM (American College of Sport Medicine)

Limit screen time (TV, computer, tablet & phone) - there are rehab centers dedicated to help reduce this addiction many people have ...

For many it is not about performance but self esteem & body image (how you look naked ☺)

Actions

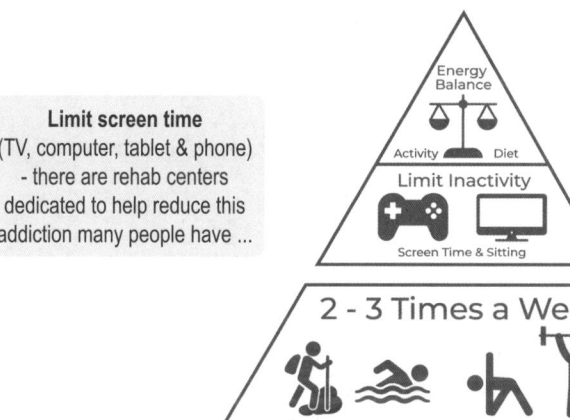

Limit all screen time and have consistent changes of body position through the entire day - Prolonged sedentary time is independently associated with negative health outcomes regardless of physical activity!

Soreness & Recovery

DOMS - delayed onset muscle soreness is theorized to be due to microscopic tears that happen in muscles at a cellular level. Pain receptors in muscles then send signals to brain and calcium builds up in muscle causing low level inflammation

- Be aware that mild DOMS is a good thing! - it shows good workout intensity - the best way to alleviate DOMS long term is to progress slowly into a new exercise program, giving muscles enough time to adapt to new stress being applied and regular massage therapy

- Rest, light motion, sleep and nutrition improve recovery (creatine, fish oil, taurine, branched chain amino acids, caffeine, citrulline malate)

- Studies show that massage, foam rolling and other manual therapies can alleviate DOMS

- Be aware that increased performance and lowered recovery time is possible with performance enhancing substances (anabolic steroids)

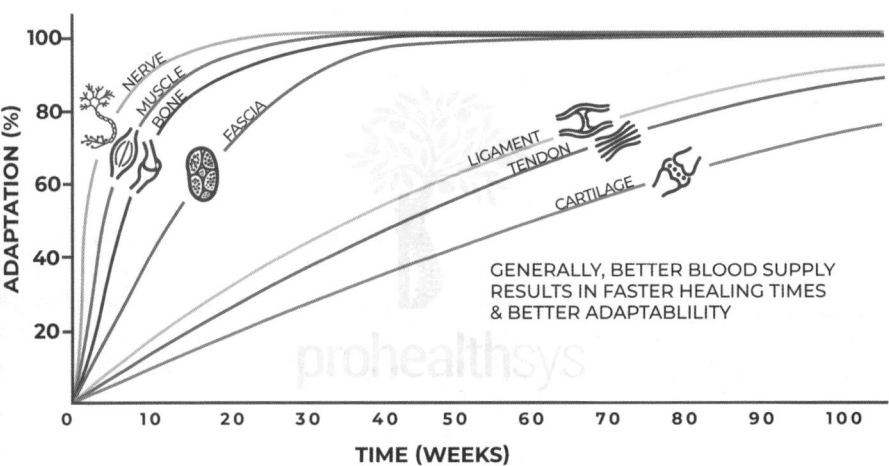

TISSUE ADAPTABILITY

(NERVE, MUSCLE, BONE, FASCIA, LIGAMENT, TENDON, CARTILAGE)

ADAPTATION (%) vs TIME (WEEKS)

GENERALLY, BETTER BLOOD SUPPLY RESULTS IN FASTER HEALING TIMES & BETTER ADAPTABLILITY

Performance increase occurs fastest during initial training as neural adaptation develops appropriate muscle firing patterns and biomechanics, then muscle hypertrophy continues as activity intensity is increased with skill. Performance enhancing substances can take athletes beyond natural genetic potential.

Detraining Effect - injury, illness, lack of motivation cause loss in performance after...

- **1-2 week for cardio** (stroke volume, work capacity, cardiac output - VO_2 max can drop by ~20% in 2 weeks - beginners lose more easily, trained athletes lose more slowly)

- **2-3 weeks for strength** and **muscle size**

- Also influenced by age, injury, overall activity level, nutrition, prior training ability

Theodorou, A. et al. (2016). Aerobic, resistance and combined training and detraining on body composition, muscle strength, lipid profile and inflammation in coronary artery disease patients. Research in Sports Medicine Vol. 24:3

Coetsee, C. Terblance, E. (2015). The time course of changes induced by resistance training and detraining on muscular and physical function in older adults. Eur Rev Aging Phys Act. 2015; 12: 7

Mujika, I.; Padilla, S.(2000), Detraining: loss of training-induced physiological and performance adaptations. Part I: short term insufficient training stimulus. Journal of Sports Med. (2), 79 – 87.

Contralateral Training Effect

- Evidence suggests by training the uninjured side, there is ↑ **gene expression** and up to a **35% strength** transfer to the injured limb

- Molecular responses to acute exercise are not confined to exercising muscles but also extend to contralateral resting muscles

- Mechanisms include motor pathway projecting & neuroplasticity to contralateral muscles to enhance performance

Catoire, M., Mensink, M., Boekschoten, M. V., Hangelbroek, R., Müller, M., Schrauwen, P., & Kersten, S. (2012). Pronounced Effects of Acute Endurance Exercise on Gene Expression in Resting and Exercising Human Skeletal Muscle. Plos ONE, 7(11), 1-10. doi:10.1371/journal

Lee, M., & Carroll, T. J. (2007). Cross Education: Possible Mechanisms for the Contralateral Effects of Unilateral Resistance Training. Sports Medicine, 37(1), 1-14. doi:10.2165/00007256-200737010-00001

There are many expert-based strategies for rehab. to target inhibited/weak muscles, relax/stretch overactive tissues.

- **Remove mechanical blockage** (tight tissues, joint dysfunction - massage, stretch, pin & stretch, contract relax, joint mobes)

- To restore functional motor control, endurance and strength, **follow the ACE protocol** during rehab.

A = **A**lign & **A**ctivate muscles with **verbal, visual & tactile** cues to bring awareness of the neuromuscular pathway that needs training

C = **C**ontrol motor function by repeating the motion with good form, avoiding recruitment

E = **E**ndurance increases by adding resistance or difficulty to build strength and further augment control and activation

There are no magic exercises ... just the ones that give the right amount of stress at the right time

Jumping Jacks   Step-Up   Punches   High Knees

Actions

Inchworm

Injury Zone
Safe Range
Injury Zone

prohealthsys

YTWL

Wall Slide

Actions

Wall Push-Up

Kneeling Push Up

Proper Technique

Breathe & focus on smooth controlled actions

Maintain neutral pelvis & do not arch back

Do movements slowly, if shaking occurs step down a level

Warning: if pain is aggravated STOP, muscle 'burn' is OK, muscle soreness over the next few days is common & normal

Outcome Measure

Working toward maintaining 2+ minutes of activity

As you build strength and endurance, progress to more challenging exercises

Prescription

_____ reps, _____ sets,

_____ seconds to hold, _____ x/day

Shoulder Taps

Hover Push Up

Tricep Dips(bent legs)

Headstand Press

Actions

Proper Technique

Breathe & focus on smooth controlled actions

Maintain neutral pelvis & do not arch back

Do movements slowly, if shaking occurs step down a level

Warning: if pain is aggravated STOP, muscle 'burn' is OK, muscle soreness over the next few days is common & normal

Outcome Measure

Working toward maintaining 2+ minutes of activity

As you build strength and endurance, progress to more challenging exercises

Prescription

_____ reps, _____ sets,

_____ seconds to hold, _____ x/day

prohealthsys

Actions

Forearms

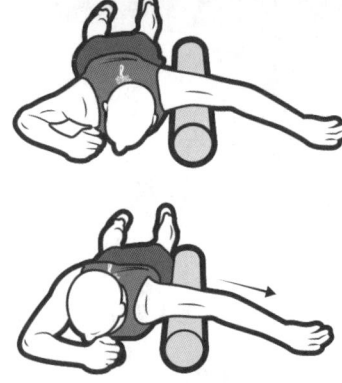

Biceps

Triceps

Shoulder Blade Reach

Proper Technique

Breathe & focus on smooth controlled actions

Maintain neutral pelvis & do not arch back

Do movements slowly, if shaking occurs step down a level

Warning: if pain is aggravated STOP, muscle 'burn' is OK, muscle soreness over the next few days is common & normal

Outcome Measure

Working toward maintaining 2+ minutes of activity

As you build strength and endurance, progress to more challenging exercises

Prescription

_____ reps, _____ sets,

_____ seconds to hold, _____ x/day

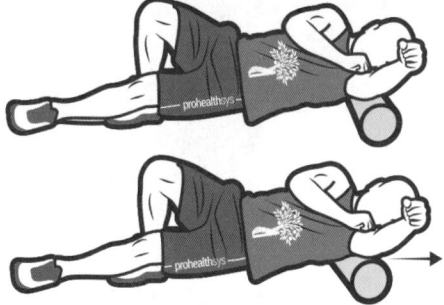

Posterior Shoulder

Shoulder Back Rotation

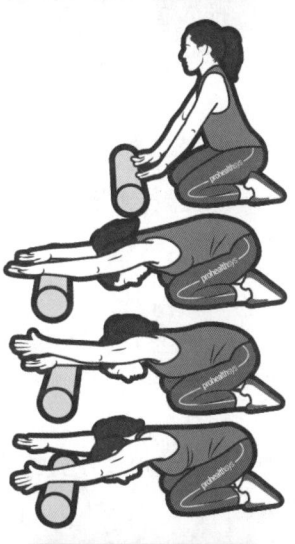

Actions

Shoulders

Shoulder Lift off

Proper Technique

Breathe & focus on smooth controlled actions

Maintain neutral pelvis & do not arch back

Do movements slowly, if shaking occurs step down a level

Warning: if pain is aggravated STOP, muscle 'burn' is OK, muscle soreness over the next few days is common & normal

Outcome Measure

Working toward maintaining 2+ minutes of activity

As you build strength and endurance, progress to more challenging exercises

Prescription

_____ reps, _____ sets,

_____ seconds to hold, _____ x/day

Actions

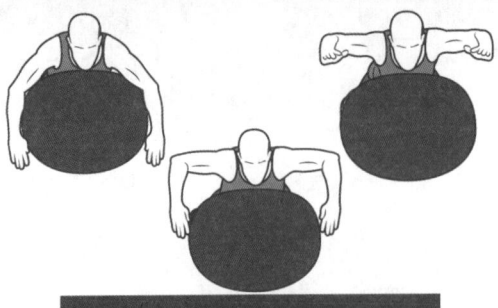

External Shoulder Rotation

Chest Press

Knee Push-Ups

One-Arm Chest Press

Incline Push-up

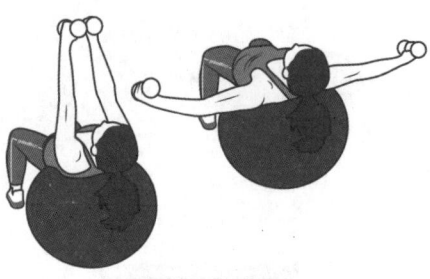

Chest Fly

Proper Technique

Breathe & focus on smooth controlled actions

Maintain neutral pelvis & do not arch back

Do movements slowly, if shaking occurs step down a level

Warning: if pain is aggravated STOP, muscle 'burn' is OK, muscle soreness over the next few days is common & normal

Outcome Measure

Working toward maintaining 2+ minutes of activity

As you build strength and endurance, progress to more challenging exercises

Prescription

_____ reps, _____ sets,

_____ seconds to hold, _____ x/day

Tricep Dip

Tricep Kickback

Lat Pullover

Reverse Fly

Decline Push-up

Plank Shoulder Taps

Actions

Proper Technique

Breathe & focus on smooth controlled actions

Maintain neutral pelvis & do not arch back

Do movements slowly, if shaking occurs step down a level

Warning: if pain is aggravated STOP, muscle 'burn' is OK, muscle soreness over the next few days is common & normal

Outcome Measure

Working toward maintaining 2+ minutes of activity

As you build strength and endurance, progress to more challenging exercises

Prescription

_____ reps, _____ sets,

_____ seconds to hold, _____ x/day

prohealthsys

Shoulder opener

Infinity spins

Shoulder spins

Actions

Proper Technique

Breathe & focus on smooth controlled actions

Maintain neutral pelvis & do not arch back

Do movements slowly, if shaking occurs step down a level

Warning: if pain is aggravated STOP, muscle 'burn' is OK, muscle soreness over the next few days is common & normal

Outcome Measure

Working toward maintaining 2+ minutes of activity

As you build strength and endurance, progress to more challenging exercises

Prescription

_____ reps, _____ sets,

_____ seconds to hold, _____ x/day

Shoulder stretch variation

Bamboo twist

Swimmer

Proper Technique

Breathe & focus on smooth controlled actions

Maintain neutral pelvis & do not arch back

Do movements slowly, if shaking occurs step down a level

Warning: if pain is aggravated STOP, muscle 'burn' is OK, muscle soreness over the next few days is common & normal

Outcome Measure

Working toward maintaining 2+ minutes of activity

As you build strength and endurance, progress to more challenging exercises

Prescription

_____ reps, _____ sets,

_____ seconds to hold, _____ x/day

prohealthsys

Actions

Shoulder Rotation

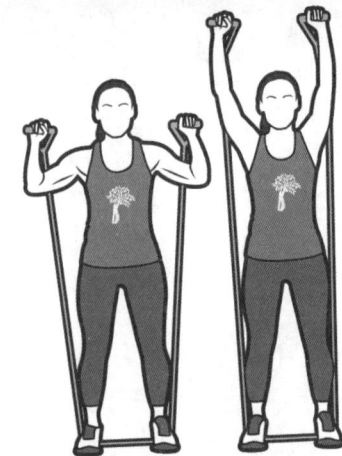

Shoulder Press

Kickback

One Arm Chest Press

Proper Technique

Breathe & focus on smooth controlled actions

Maintain neutral pelvis & do not arch back

Do movements slowly, if shaking occurs step down a level

Warning: if pain is aggravated STOP, muscle 'burn' is OK, muscle soreness over the next few days is common & normal

Outcome Measure

Working toward maintaining 2+ minutes of activity

As you build strength and endurance, progress to more challenging exercises

Prescription

_____ reps, _____ sets,

_____ seconds to hold, _____ x/day

prohealthsys

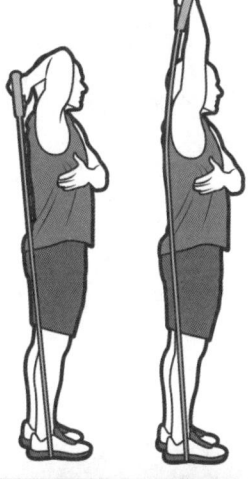

Tricep Extension

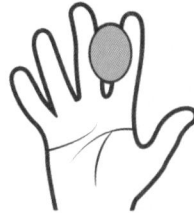

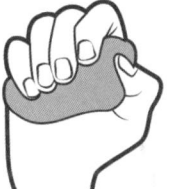
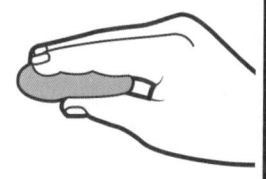

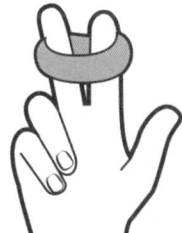

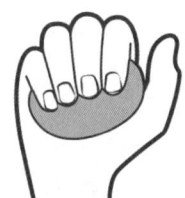

Actions

Proper Technique

Breathe & focus on smooth controlled actions

Maintain neutral pelvis & do not arch back

Do movements slowly, if shaking occurs step down a level

Warning: if pain is aggravated STOP, muscle 'burn' is OK, muscle soreness over the next few days is common & normal

Outcome Measure

Working toward maintaining 2+ minutes of activity

As you build strength and endurance, progress to more challenging exercises

Prescription

_____ reps, _____ sets,

_____ seconds to hold, _____ x/day

prohealthsys

Actions

Arm Rotation

Wrist Curl

Alt.Shoulder Press

Goblet Thruster

Proper Technique

Breathe & focus on smooth controlled actions

Maintain neutral pelvis & do not arch back

Do movements slowly, if shaking occurs step down a level

Warning: if pain is aggravated STOP, muscle 'burn' is OK, muscle soreness over the next few days is common & normal

Outcome Measure

Working toward maintaining 2+ minutes of activity

As you build strength and endurance, progress to more challenging exercises

Prescription

_____ reps, _____ sets,

_____ seconds to hold, _____ x/day

prohealthsys

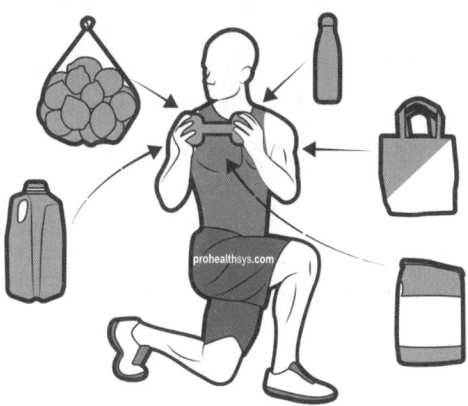

Single Leg Scarecrow

Lunge and Curl

Skull Crusher

Actions

Proper Technique

Breathe & focus on smooth controlled actions

Maintain neutral pelvis & do not arch back

Do movements slowly, if shaking occurs step down a level

Warning: if pain is aggravated STOP, muscle 'burn' is OK, muscle soreness over the next few days is common & normal

Outcome Measure

Working toward maintaining 2+ minutes of activity

As you build strength and endurance, progress to more challenging exercises

Prescription

_____ reps, _____ sets,

_____ seconds to hold, _____ x/day

prohealthsys

One Arm Chest Press

Crossing Clutch Curl

Tricep Press

Shoulder Rotation

Actions

Proper Technique

Breathe & focus on smooth controlled actions

Maintain neutral pelvis & do not arch back

Do movements slowly, if shaking occurs step down a level

Warning: if pain is aggravated STOP, muscle 'burn' is OK, muscle soreness over the next few days is common & normal

Outcome Measure

Working toward maintaining 2+ minutes of activity

As you build strength and endurance, progress to more challenging exercises

Prescription

_____ reps, _____ sets,

_____ seconds to hold, _____ x/day

prohealthsys

Front Circle

One Arm Russian Swing

Plyo Push up

Halo

Actions

Proper Technique

Breathe & focus on smooth controlled actions

Maintain neutral pelvis & do not arch back

Do movements slowly, if shaking occurs step down a level

Warning: if pain is aggravated STOP, muscle 'burn' is OK, muscle soreness over the next few days is common & normal

Outcome Measure

Working toward maintaining 2+ minutes of activity

As you build strength and endurance, progress to more challenging exercises

Prescription

_____ reps, _____ sets,

_____ seconds to hold, _____ x/day

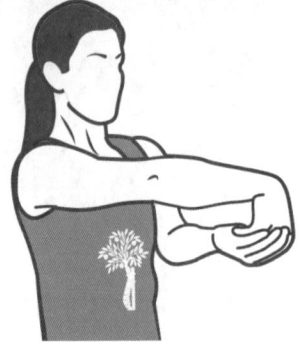

Actions

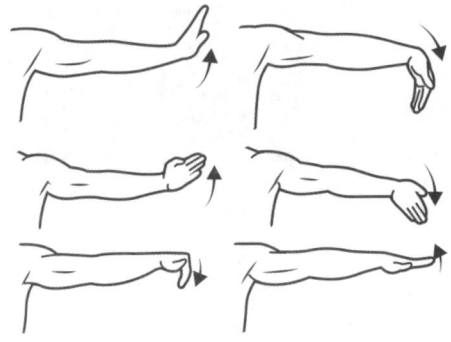

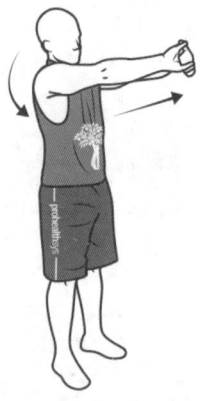

Proper Technique

Breathe & focus on smooth controlled actions

Maintain neutral pelvis & do not arch back

Do movements slowly, if shaking occurs step down a level

Warning: if pain is aggravated STOP, muscle 'burn' is OK, muscle soreness over the next few days is common & normal

Outcome Measure

Working toward maintaining 2+ minutes of activity

As you build strength and endurance, progress to more challenging exercises

Prescription

_____ reps, _____ sets,

_____ seconds to hold, _____ x/day

prohealthsys

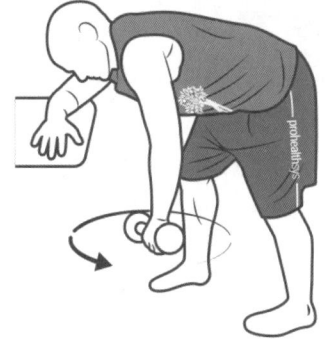
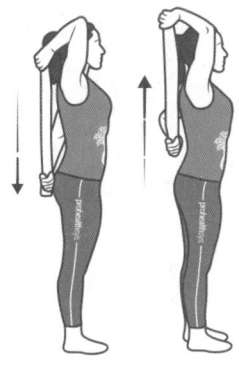

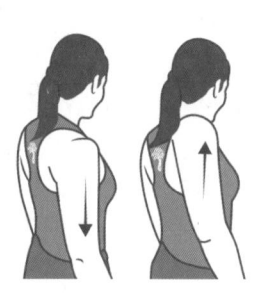
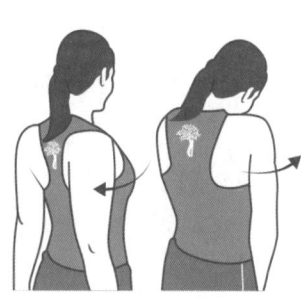

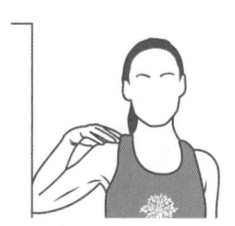
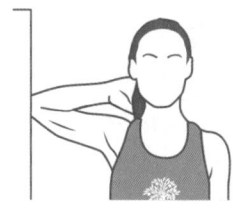

Actions

Proper Technique

Breathe & focus on smooth controlled actions

Maintain neutral pelvis & do not arch back

Do movements slowly, if shaking occurs step down a level

Warning: if pain is aggravated STOP, muscle 'burn' is OK, muscle soreness over the next few days is common & normal

Outcome Measure

Working toward maintaining 2+ minutes of activity

As you build strength and endurance, progress to more challenging exercises

Prescription

_____ reps, _____ sets,

_____ seconds to hold, _____ x/day

Actions

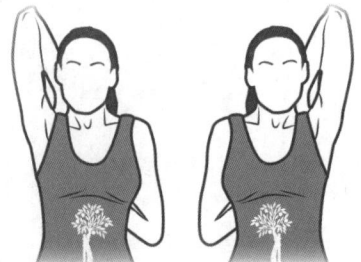

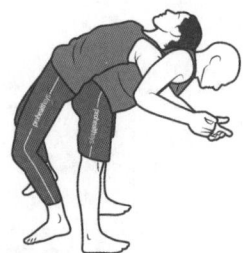

Mini Back Pack

Proper Technique

Breathe & focus on smooth controlled actions

Maintain neutral pelvis & do not arch back

Do movements slowly, if shaking occurs step down a level

Warning: if pain is aggravated STOP, muscle 'burn' is OK, muscle soreness over the next few days is common & normal

Outcome Measure

Working toward maintaining 2+ minutes of activity

As you build strength and endurance, progress to more challenging exercises

Prescription

_____ reps, _____ sets,

_____ seconds to hold, _____ x/day

Warrior II

Pyramid

Bridge

Thread the Needle

Downward-Facing Dog

Bow

Actions

Proper Technique

Breathe & focus on smooth controlled actions

Maintain neutral pelvis & do not arch back

Do movements slowly, if shaking occurs step down a level

Warning: if pain is aggravated STOP, muscle 'burn' is OK, muscle soreness over the next few days is common & normal

Outcome Measure

Working toward maintaining 2+ minutes of activity

As you build strength and endurance, progress to more challenging exercises

Prescription

_____ reps, _____ sets,

_____ seconds to hold, _____ x/day

The effectiveness of massage therapy - a summary of evidence based research review of over 14,296 articles suggests massage therapy is an evidence-based therapeutic modality effective for managing...

Stress, anxiety, depression and relaxation [1-12]

Relaxation is one of the reasons massage works so well and helps reduce depression and anxiety.[1-12] One study showed massage therapy may reduce blood pressure and helps people to sleep, even when they are under the unusual stresses of hospital care.[7] A Korean study (Jane et. al.) showed massage was more helpful for patients with the deep pain of bone cancer than receiving compassionate attention.[12]

Pain reduction [13-19, 28, 30-31] and improved sleep [20-22]

Pain reduction is one of the main themes of massage therapy therapeutic benefits; and it works in a similar way as our natural instinct to "rub away the pain" whenever we hurt ourselves (that hurt can be both physical or psychological in nature). Munk et al. showed **decreased pain in older adults with persistent pain**. Other research by Hernadez et al showed for low back pain, the massage therapy group, as compared to the relaxation group, reported experiencing **less pain, depression, anxiety and improved sleep**. They also showed improved trunk and pain flexion performance, and their serotonin and dopamine levels were higher.[14]

Improved ROM [23-28]

Competent massage therapists are taught the benefit of early mobilization and range of motion exercises because they help people get better faster. **The evidence strongly suggests recovery from nearly any injury or surgery is greatly facilitated by early mobilization**. It is good practice as part of assessment and therapy to take all patients through AROM with every visit.

Chronic neck pain and headaches [34-41]

Chronic neck pain and headaches are among the most common reasons people choose massage therapy. In the clinical journal of Pain, Sherman et al. produced an RCT for the treatment of neck pain. At 10 weeks, more participants randomized to massage experienced clinically significant improvement on the neck disability index (NDI); differences between groups were strongest at 4 weeks and not evident by 26 weeks, with no negative side-effects. This research suggests that massage was safe and may have clinical benefits for treating chronic neck pain at least in the short term.[38] **Cook et al, performed an RTC to and found that follow up visits ("booster dose") had improvements in both dysfunction and pain at 12 weeks**.[39] Moraska et al, evaluated tension type headaches with massage therapy and found reduced perceived headache pain and frequency for massage therapy vs placebo or wait-list groups and pressure-pain threshold improved in all muscles tested for massage only.[40]

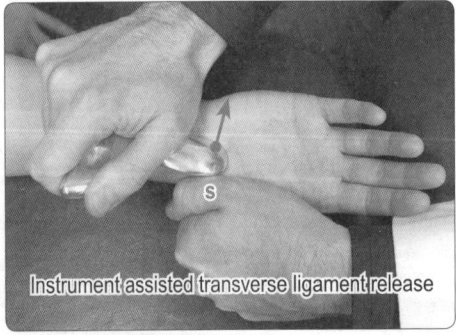

Instrument assisted transverse ligament release

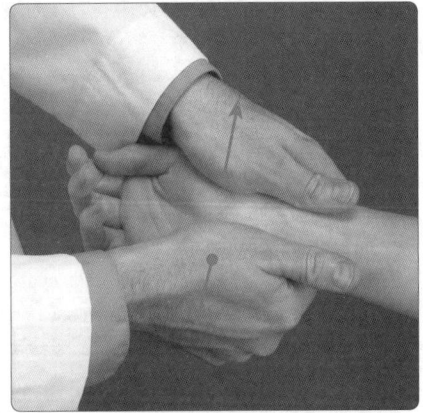

Actions

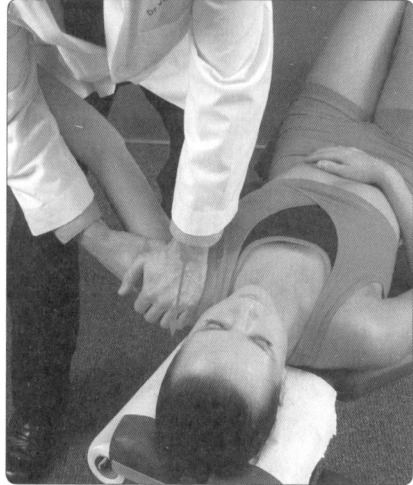
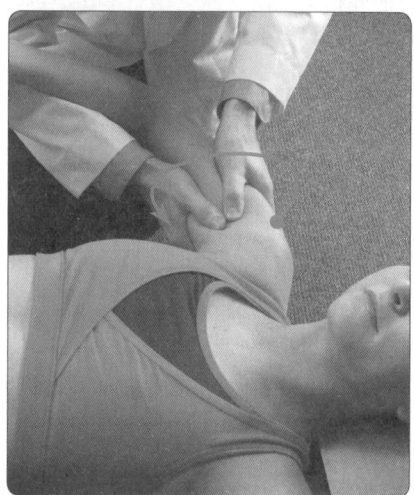

Wrist Supination Restriction MET

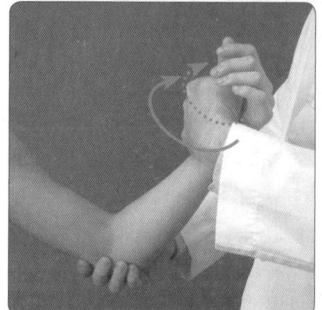
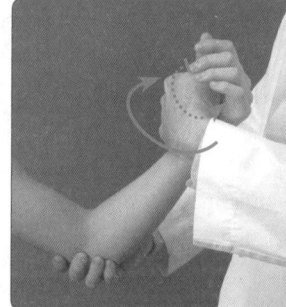
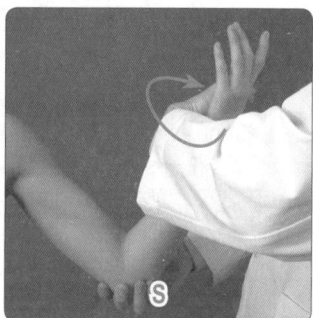

Supination tissue resistance | Patient contracts ~10% in pronation | Clinician finds new end range

Actions

Learn more

EVIDENCE-BASED

JOINT-PLAY and MOBILIZATION

Joint play, mobilization, palpation, ROM,
goniometry & exercise rehab.
Companion online quizzes, videos and more...
Dr. Nikita A. Vizniak, DC

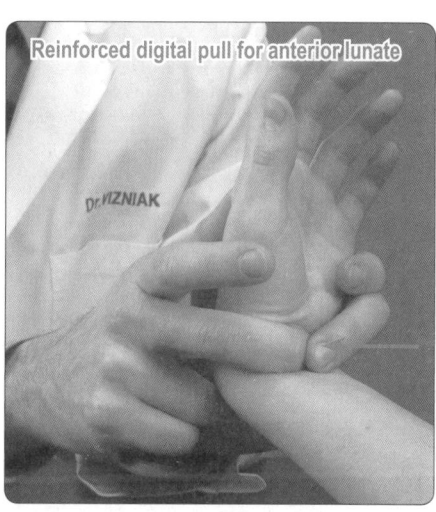

Reinforced digital pull for anterior lunate

Dr. VIZNIAK

Acupuncture is a Traditional Chinese Medicine practice that involves the insertion of filiform (hair-thin) needles into specific points on the body (acupuncture points). There are **~365 acupuncture points** on the human body that connects **20 meridians** (aka pathways), running along the full length of the body. The 20 meridians can be divided into **12 main meridians and 8 extra meridians** and these meridians are what connect the skin with internal organs and muscles. Because of this connection, the meridians allow for the flow of qi (energy) that is responsible for optimal health.

Physical pain conditions (such as arm pain) is due to the stagnation/poor flow of qi, needling specific acupuncture points aids in re-establishing the smooth flow of qi and therefore treats pain. Point selection is based on the following criteria:

1. **Acupuncture point indication/ action** - E.g. BL 60 – relaxes sinews & strengthens the neck, reduces pain

2. **Which meridian is the pain affecting?** Du, Bladder, and Gallbladder meridian are all affected by neck pain

3. **Where are the pain points?** - "Ashi" points are specific points of pain elicited with palpation that can be needled to alleviate the pain

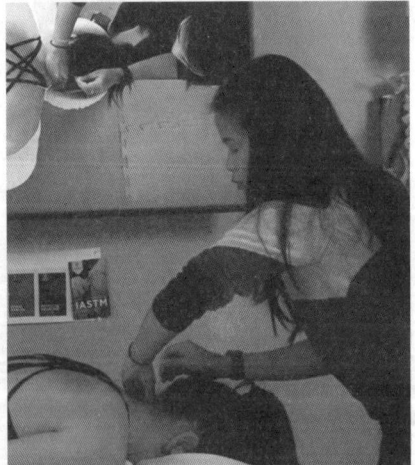

Electric current can be attached to the needles to stimulate the specific points/muscles. This will make the effects of the acupuncture points more strong and increase the release of pain relieving peptides (opioid peptides -enkephalins, endorphins, and dysnorphins).

- Lower frequencies (2 hz – 30hz) will stimulate enkephalin release

- Higher frequencies (>30 hz) will stimulate dysnorphins

Treatment course

The average number of acupuncture treatments for resolution of pain ranges from 4 – 12 treatments. These treatments should be a maximum 1-week apart, although for more expedited results having 2 – 3 treatments per week would be ideal. Each treatment lasts 30 – 45 minutes and may/may not involve electroacupuncture. Depending on the style of acupuncture practiced, improvements should be seen in 1 – 3 treatments and will last longer the more treatments received.

Acupuncture should be part a complete holistic treatment plan. Obstacles such as structural issues (e.g. lumbar radiculopathy, disc herniation) and inflammation (due to diet, smoking, stress) will impede in complete resolution of pain. So long as these obstacles are in place, acupuncture will only help short-term for pain management.

The ideal candidate for acupuncture is someone who:

- Has a health care team which includes chiropractor, PT, RMT/LMT, and MD

- Is willing to make changes in their lifestyle (diet, smoking, stress)

- Has a positive attitude towards their health outcomes

- Unable or does not want to take opioid medications or other pain medications

prohealthsys

Prolotherapy is a regenerative injection technique designed to stimulate healing. The injection consists of dextrose and a local anaesthetic creating a proliferant sugar water solution. Many different types of musculoskeletal injuries and pain may be successfully treated with prolotherapy including low back and neck pain, chronic sprains/strains, whiplash injuries, golfer's/tennis elbow, knee, ankle, shoulder or joint pain such as osteoarthritis. Prolotherapy works by stimulating healing and growth factors to promote tissue repair in a specific injured area. It can be used in either sub acute or chronic cases, even if the pain has been present for years – provided the patient is healthy and heals well.

Prolotherapy works by causing temporary, low grade inflammation at the site of ligament or tendon weakness (fibro-osseous junction), pushing the body into a healing cascade. Fibroblasts become active which helps synthesize collagen fibers, thereby strengthening connective tissue in the area of injury. This inflammatory stimulus resumes or initiates a new connective tissue repair cascade to either begin or finish a repair sequence that was started but never completed.

Prolotherapy should be considered as non surgical option for treating low back pain following cases that:

- Physical therapy care doesn't resolve concern

- Ligament structures are tender on examination

- Pain is less when mobile. (The patient is in less pain while in motion, but they hurt more when still or on arising in the morning)

Treatment course

The average number of treatments needed is between 4-6, with some people needing more and some needing less. Prolotherapy can also be used for those with failed back surgery but these cases will likely take longer. Improvements should be seen by the second or third treatment with subsequent improvement as you continue. If no improvement after 4 treatments there should be a reevaluation for interfering factors such as poor sleep, diet, continued aggravating activities, illness, or use of anti inflammatory medicines that inhibit healing.

The Ideal Prolotherapy Candidate Has The Following:

- Pain originating from a ligament, tendon, or joint

- Strong immune system

- Great attitude and mental outlook

- Willingness to improve and receive follow-up visits

- Non smoker

- Has great nutritional status

- Sleeps and recovers well

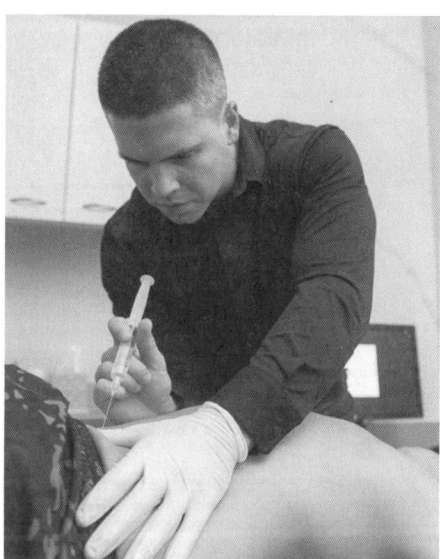

Actions

Actions

Respected food writer Michael Pollan says everything he's learned about food and health can be summed up in seven words: **"Eat food, not too much, mostly plants."** Eat real food -- vegetables, fruits, whole grains, and, yes, fish and natural organic meats and **avoid "edible food-like substances."** There is no need to over complicate the science, the hard part is sticking to the regime and finding good food sources. Here are some words of advice:

1. **Don't eat anything your great grand parents wouldn't recognize as food.** "When you pick up that box of cookies, or eat something with 15 ingredients you can't pronounce, ask yourself, "What are those things doing there?"

2. **Don't eat anything with more than 5 ingredients, or ingredients you can't pronounce.**

3. Bacteria eat real food, so should you. **Don't eat anything that won't eventually rot.** "There are exceptions -- honey -- but as a rule, things like Twinkies that never go bad aren't food."

4. **Always leave the table a little hungry,"** Pollan says. "Many cultures have rules that you stop eating before you are full. In Japan, they say eat until you are four-fifths full. Islamic culture has a similar rule, and in German culture they say, 'Tie off the sack before it's full.'"

5. **Families traditionally ate together, around a table and not a TV, at regular meal times.** It's a good tradition. **Enjoy meals with the people you love.**

Nutrition & Feeding Window

- **"Feeding window" = within 1 hr after class**

- Research shows, immediately after workout insulin levels spike rapidly for a few hours priming the body for synthesizing new muscle, limiting exercise-induced muscle loss, and restoring energy levels - consuming **20-40g of protein within 2 hrs following workout significantly increases muscle growth**

1. Stark M, Lukaszuk J, Prawitz A, Salacinski A. Protein timing and its effects on muscular hypertrophy and strength in individuals engaged in weight-training. Journal of the International Society of Sports Nutrition. 2012;9:54. doi:10.1186/1550-2783-9-54.
2. Kerksick C, Harvey T, Stout J, Campbell B, Wilborn C, Kreider R, Kalman D, Ziegenfuss T, Lopez H, Landis J, Ivy JL, Antonio J: International Society of Sports Nutrition position stand: nutrient timing. J Int Soc Sports Nutr. 2008, 5: 17-10.1186/1550-2783-5-17.

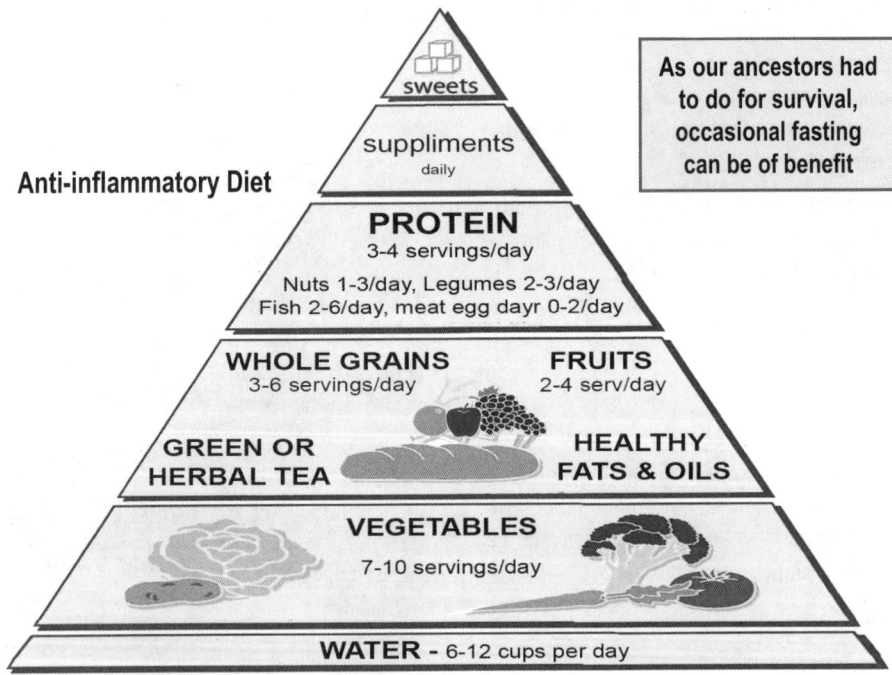

Anti-inflammatory Diet

As our ancestors had to do for survival, occasional fasting can be of benefit

sweets

suppliments
daily

PROTEIN
3-4 servings/day

Nuts 1-3/day, Legumes 2-3/day
Fish 2-6/day, meat egg dayr 0-2/day

WHOLE GRAINS
3-6 servings/day

FRUITS
2-4 serv/day

GREEN OR HERBAL TEA

HEALTHY FATS & OILS

VEGETABLES
7-10 servings/day

WATER - 6-12 cups per day

'Those who think they have no time for healthy eating…will sooner or later have to find time for illness.' - Edward Stanley

prohealthsys

Eat less CRAP:

 C - carbonated drinks

 R - refined sugar

 A - artificial sweeteners & colors

 P - processed foods

Eat more FOOD:

 F - fruits & veggies

 O - organic lean proteins

 O - omega 3 fatty acids

 D - drink water

Actions

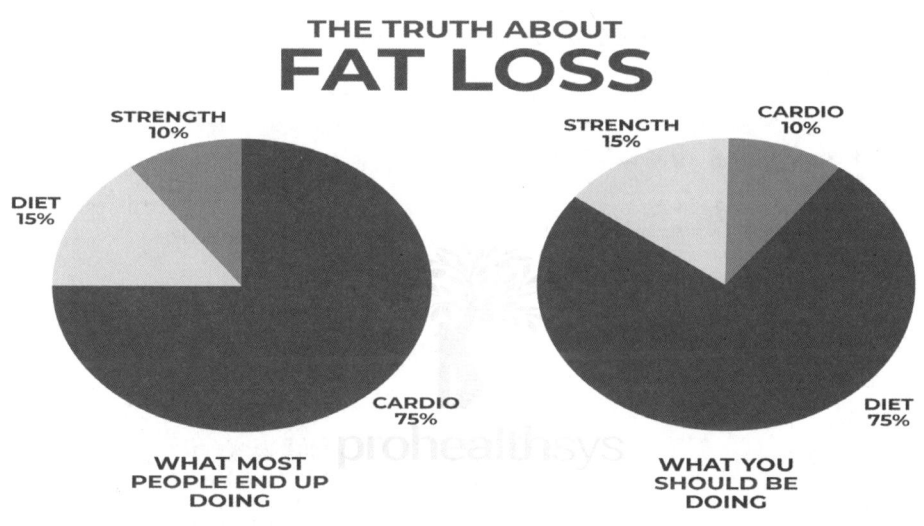

THE TRUTH ABOUT
FAT LOSS

WHAT MOST PEOPLE END UP DOING: STRENGTH 10%, DIET 15%, CARDIO 75%

WHAT YOU SHOULD BE DOING: STRENGTH 15%, CARDIO 10%, DIET 75%

Carbs Energy = 4 kcal/g

Age Group	RDA (g/d)	AMDR (%)
Infant (0-1 yr)	60-90 g/d	n/a
Child (1-8 yrs)	130 g/d	45-65%
Adolescent (9-16 yrs)		
Males (>17 yrs)		
Females (>17 yrs)		
Pregnancy	175 g/d	
Lactation	210 g/d	

Basic Carbohydrate Metabolism
- Carbohydrates (CHOs) are composed of only hydrogen, carbon & oxygen & are the building blocks of all other biological material

Protein Energy = 4 kcal/g

Age Group	RDA (g/d)	AMDR (%)
Infant (0-1 yr)	13.5 g/d	n/a
Child (1-8 yrs)	18 g/d	10-30%
Adolescent (9-16 yrs)	40 g/d	
Males (>17 yrs)	56 g/d	10-35%
Females (>17 yrs)	46 g/d	
Pregnancy	71 g/d	
Lactation		

Basic Metabolism

- Digestion **via** hydrochloric acid & pepsin; pancreatic & intestinal proteases.

- Absorption occurs mainly in SI where they are broken down & absorbed as single **amino acids**

- Protein synthesis (anabolism), degradation to urea (catabolism) occurs continuously with excess stored as fat

Protein requirement per kg based on age

0-1 yrs	1-3 yrs	4-13 yrs	14-18 yrs	Adults	Pregnancy
1.5 g/kg/day	1.1 g/kg/day	0.95 g/kg/day	0.85 g/kg/day	**0.8 g/kg/day**	1.1 g/kg/day

Fat Energy = 9 kcal/g

Age Group	RDA (g/d)	AMDR
Infant (0-1 yr)	30 g/d	30-40%
Child (1-8 yrs)	n/a	25-35%
Adolescent (9-16 yrs)		
Males (>17 yrs)		
Females (>17 yrs)		
Pregnancy		
Lactation		

Recommended intake: < 30% of daily caloric intake, < 10% as saturated fat

Basic metabolism

- Triglycerides (TG) = 90% of fat in diet
- Cholesterol 5%, phospholipids 4%
- Fat soluble vitamins - A, D, E, K

  Digestion highlights - pancreatic lipase, bile acids, micelle formation

- Transportation - as lipoproteins (HDL, LDL, VLDL)

Actions

prohealthsys

Carbs

The Body's Primary Source of Energy

4 kcal/g

Protein

Building Block of Tissue

4 kcal/g

Fats

The Body's Insulator and Energy source

9 kcal/g

Function (Carbs)

✔ Carbs are the body's prefered energy source.

✔ Every cell and tissue in the body can use glucose(simple form carbohydrate) for energy

✔ Prevents the body from using protein as an energy source.

✔ Dietary fibres in carbs contribute to the overall health of the colon and some play a role in regulating blood sugar levels.

Function (Protein)

✔ Essential for the growth and repair of tissue

✔ Important for making hormones and enzymes.

✔ Can be used as an energy source when energy from carbs is limited.

✔ Every cell in the body contains protein and is used in the formation of many molecules essential for life.

Function (Fats)

✔ Helps the absorption of fat-soluble vitamins (A, E, E, & K)

✔ Insulates the body

✔ Helps the body store energy. Excess fat storage may lead to health complications.

✔ Essential fats play an important role in basic metabolism, and may help prevent heart disease.

Actions

Good Source (Carbs)

Rye Bread

Quinoa

Oats

Whole Grain Bread

Fruits

Beans

Sweet Potatoes

Navy Beans

Bran Flakes

Pinto Beans

Oatmeal

Whole Grain Pasta

Lentils

TIP: KEEP IT HIGH FIBRE!

Good Source (Protein)

Almonds

Nuts

Seeds

Chicken

Tofu

Beans

Fish

Soy Beans

Kidney Beans

Eggs

Turkey

Peanuts

Navy Beans

TIP: KEEP IT LEAN!

Good Source (Fats)

Walnuts

Soybean oil

Fish

Tuna

Flax seed

Salmon

Sesame seeds

Avocado

Trout

Peanuts

Olive Oil

Almonds

TIP: LIMIT ANIMAL SOURCES

References

1. Vizniak NA. Clinical Cadaver Dissections. 1999-2021
2. Abrams GD, Safran MR: Diagnosis and management of superior labrum anterior osterior lesions in overhead athletes. Br J Sports Med 44:311–318, 2010.
3. Adson AW, Coffey JR: Cervical rib: a method of anterior approach for relief of symptoms by division of the scalenus anticus. Ann Surg 85:839–857, 1927.
4. Alberta FG, El Attrache NS, Bissell S, et al: The development and validcation of a functional assessment tool for the upper extremity in the overhead athlete. Am J Sports Med 38:903–911, 2010.
5. Alqunaee M, Galvin R, Fahey T. Diagnostic accuracy of clinical tests for subacromial impingement syndrome: a systematic review and meta-analysis. Arch Phys Med Rehabil. 2012 Feb. 93(2):229-36.
6. Altchek DA, Warren RF, Skyhar MJ, et al: T-plasty: a technique for treating multidirectional instability in the athlete. J Bone Joint Surg Am 73:105–112, 1991.
7. Anderson MW, Brennan C, Mittal A: Imaging evaluation of the rotator cuff. Clin Sports Med 31:605– 631, 2012.
8. Andrews JA, Timmerman LA, Wilk KE: Baseball. In Pettrone FA, editor: Athletic injuries of the shoulder, New York, 1995, McGraw-Hill.
9. Andrews JR, Gillogly S: Physical examination of the shoulder in throwing athletes. In Zarins B, Andrews JR, Carson WG, editors: Injuries to the throwing arm, Philadelphia, 1985, WB Saunders.
10. Arcand MA, Reider B: Shoulder and upper arm. In Reider B, editor: The orthopedic physical examination, Philadelphia, 1999, WB Saunders.
11. Arroyo JS, Flatow EL: Management of rotator cuff disease: intact and repairable cuff. In Iannotti JP, Williams GR, editors: Disorders of the shoulder, Philadelphia, 1999, Lippincott Williams & Wilkins.
12. Atasoy E: Thoracic outlet compression syndrome. Orthop Clin North Am 27:265–303, 1996.
13. Ault J, Suutala K: Thoracic outlet syndrome. J Man Manip Ther 6:118–129, 1998.
14. Aval SM, Durand P, Shankwiler JA: Neurovascular injuries to the athlete's shoulder: part II. J Am Acad Orthop Surg 15:281–289, 2007.
15. Aval SM, Durand P, Shankwiler JA: Neurovascular injuries to the athlete's shoulder: part I. J Am Acad Orthop Surg 15:249–256, 2007.
16. Axe MJ: Acromioclavicular joint injuries in the athlete. Sports Med Arthro Rev 8:182–191, 2000.
17. Baker CL, Liu SH: Neurovascular injuries to the shoulder. J Orthop Sports Phys Ther 18:360–364, 1993.
18. Barth JR, Burkhart SS, DeBeer JF: The bear-hug test: a new and sensitive test for diagnosing a subscapularis tear. Arthroscopy 22:1076–1084, 2006.
19. Bearden JM, Hughston JC, Whatley GS: Acromioclavicular dislocation: method of treatment. J Sports Med 1:5–17, 1973.
20. Beaton D, Richards RR: Assessing the reliability and responsiveness of 5 shoulder questionnaires. J Shoulder Elbow Surg 7(6):565–572, 1998.
21. Beaton DE, Katz JN, Fossel AH, et al: Measuring the whole or the parts? Validity, reliability, and responsiveness of the disabilities of the arm, shoulder and hand outcome measure in different regions of the upper extremity. J Hand Ther 14:128–146, 2001.
22. Beaton DE, Wright JG, Katz JN: Upper extremity collaborative group. Development of the Quick DASH: comparison of three item reduction approaches. J Bone Joint Surg Am 87:1038–1046, 2005.
23. Behun MA, Geeslin AG, O'Hagan EC, King JC. Partial Tears of the Distal Biceps Brachii Tendon: A Systematic Review of Surgical Outcomes. J Hand Surg Am. 2016 Jul. 41 (7):e175-89.
24. Bell RH, Noble JB: Biceps disorders. In Hawkins RJ, Misamore GW, editors: Shoulder injuries in the athlete, New York, 1996, Churchill Livingstone.
25. Bencardino JT, Rosenberg ZS: Entrapment neuropathies of the shoulder and elbow in the athlete. Clin Sports Med 25:465–488, 2006.
26. Bennett WF: Specificity of the Speed's test: arthroscopic technique for evaluating the biceps tendon at the level of the bicipital groove. Arthroscopy 14:789–796, 1998.
27. Bennett WF: Specificity of the speed's test: arthroscopic technique for evaluating the biceps tendon at the level of the bicipital groove. Arthroscopy 14:789–796, 1998.
28. Berg EE, Ciullo JV: A clinical test for superior glenoid labral or "SLAP" lesions. Clin J Sports Med 8:121– 123, 1998.
29. Bernageau J: Roentgenographic assessment of the rotator cuff. Clin Orthop 254:87–91, 1990.
30. Bertelli JA, Ghizoni MF: Long thoracic nerve: anatomy and functional assessment. J Bone Joint Surg Am 87:993–998, 2005.
31. Beyzadeoglu T, Circi E. Superior Labrum Anterior Posterior Lesions and Associated Injuries: Return to Play in Elite Athletes. Orthop J Sports Med. 2015 Apr. 3 (4):2325967115577359.
32. Bigliani LH, Morrison DS, April EW: The morphology of the acromion and its relation to rotator cuff tears. Orthop Trans 10:228, 1986.
33. Bigliani LU, Codd TP, Conner PM, et al: Shoulder motion and laxity in the professional baseball player. Am J Sports Med 25:609–613, 1997.
34. Bigliani LU, Kelkar R, Flatow EL, et al: Glenohumeral stability: biomechanical properties of passive and active stabilizers. Clin Orthop Relat Res 330:13–30, 1996.
35. Bigliani LU, Levine WN: Subacromial impingement syndrome. J Bone Joint Surg Am 79:1854–1868, 1997.
36. Bigliani LU, Tucker JB, Flatow EL, et al: The relationship of acromial architecture to rotator cuff disease. Clin Sports Med 10:823–838, 1991.
37. Blasier RB, Guldberg RE, Rothman ED: Anterior shoulder stability: contributions of rotator cuff forces and the capsular ligaments in a cadaver model. J Shoulder Elbow Surg 1:140–150, 1992.
38. Bonsell S, Pearsall AW, Heitman RJ, et al: The relationship of age, gender and degenerative changes observed on radiographs of the shoulder in asymptomatic individuals. J Bone Joint Surg Br 82:1135–1139, 2000.
39. Bonutti PM, Norfray JF, Friedman RJ, et al: Kinematic MRI of the shoulder. J Comput Assist Tomogr 17:666–669, 1993.
40. Boody SG, Freedman L, Waterland JC: Shoulder movements during abduction in the scapular plane. Arch Phys Med Rehabil 51:595–604, 1970.
41. Borsa PA, Jacobson JA, Scibek JS, et al: Comparison of dynamic sonography to stress radiography for assessing glenohumeral laxity in asymptomatic shoulders. Am J Sports Med 33(5):734–741, 2005.
42. Borsa PA, Laudner KG, Sauers EL: Mobility and stability adaptations in the shoulder of the overhead athlete—a theoretical and evidence-based perspective. Sports Med 38:17–36, 2008.
43. Borsa PA, Sauers EL, Herling DE: Patterns of glenohumeral joint laxity and stiffness in healthy men and women. Med Sci Sports Exerc 32:1685–1690, 2000.
44. Borsa PA, Scibek JS, Jacobson JA, et al: Sonographic stress measurement of glenohumeral joint laxity in collegiate swimmers and age matched controls. Am J Sports Med 33:1077–1084, 2005.
45. Boublik M, Silliman JF: History and physical examination. In Hawkins RJ, Misamore GW, editors: Shoulder injuries in the athlete, New York, 1996, Churchill Livingstone.
46. Bowen M, Warren R: Ligamentous control of shoulder stability based on selective cutting and static translation. Clin Sports Med 10:757–782, 1991.
47. Boyd EA, Torrance GM: Clinical measures of shoulder subluxation: their reliability. Can J Public Health 83(Suppl 2):S24–S28, 1992.
48. Boyle JJ: Is the pain and dysfunction of shoulder impingement lesion really second rib syndrome in disguise? Two case reports. Manual Therapy 4:44– 48, 1999.
49. Branch TP, Lawton RL, Jobst CA, et al: The role of glenohumeral capsular ligaments in internal and external rotation of the humerus. Am J Sports Med 23:632–637, 1995.
50. Braun S, Kokmeyer D, Millett PJ: Shoulder injuries in the throwing athlete. J Bone Joint Surg Am 91:966–978, 2009.
51. Breckenridge JD, McAuley JH: Shoulder pain and disability index (SPADI). J Physiotherapy 57(3):197, 2011.
52. Brophy RH, Beauvais RL, Jones EC, et al: Measurement of shoulder activity level. Clin Orthop Relat Res 439:101–108, 2005.
53. Brossmann J, Preidler KW, Pedowitz KA, et al: Shoulder impingement syndrome: Influence of shoulder position on rotator cuff impingement: an anatomic study. Am J Roentgenol 167:1511–1515, 1992.
54. Brown C: Compressive, invasive referred pain to the shoulder. Clin Orthop 173:55–62, 1983.
55. Brown GA, Tan JL, Kirkley A: The lax shoulders in females. Clin Orthop Relat Res 372:110–122, 2000.
56. Brunnstrom S: Muscle testing around the shoulder girdle: a study of the function of shoulder blade fixators in 17 cases of shoulder paralysis. J Bone Joint Surg Am 23:263–272, 1941.
57. Buchberger DJ: Introduction of a new physical examination procedure for the differentiation of acromioclavicular joint lesions and subacromial impingement. J Manip Physio Ther 22:316–321, 1999.
58. Burkhart SS, Morgan CD, Kibler WB: Shoulder injuries in overhead athletes: the "dead arm" revisited. Clin Sports Med 19:125–158, 2000.
59. Burkhart SS, Morgan CD, Kibler WB: The disabled throwing shoulder: spectrum of pathology, part one: pathoanatomy and biomechanics. Arthroscopy 19:404–420, 2003.
60. Burkhart SS, Morgan CD, Kibler WB: The disabled throwing shoulder: spectrum of pathology, part three: the SICK scapula, scapular dyskinesia, the kinetic chain, and rehabilitation. Arthroscopy 19:641–661, 2003.
61. Burkhart SS, Morgan CD, Kibler WB: The disabled throwing shoulder: spectrum of pathology, part two: evaluation and treatment of SLAP lesions in throwers. Arthroscopy 19:531–539, 2003.
62. Burkhart SS, Morgan CD: The peel-back mechanism—its role in producing and extending posterior type II SLAP lesions and its effect on SLAP repair rehabilitation. Arthroscopy 14:637–640, 1998.
63. Burkhart SS: Recurrent anterior shoulder instability. In Norris TR, editor: Orthopedic knowledge update: shoulder and elbow, Rosemont, IL, 2002, American Academy of Orthopedic Surgeons.
64. Butcher JD, Siekanowicz A, Pettrone F: Pectoralis major rupture: ensuring accurate diagnosis and effective rehabilitation. Phys Sportsmed 24:37–44, 1996.
65. Butler DS: Mobilisation of the nervous system, Melbourne, 1991, Churchill Livingstone.
66. Butters KP: Nerve lesions of the shoulder. In De Lee, JC, Drez D, editors: Orthopedic sports medicine: principles and practice, Philadelphia, 1994, WB Saunders.
67. Cadet ER: Evaluation of glenohumeral instability. Orthop Clin North Am 41:287–295, 2010.
68. Cadogan A, Laslett M, Hing W, et al: Interexaminer reliability of orthopedic special tests used in the assessment of shoulder pain. Manual Therapy 16:131–135, 2011.
69. Caekebeke P, Vermeersch N, Duerinckx J, van Riet R: Radiological and Clinical Evaluation of the Transosseous Cortical Button Technique in Distal Biceps Tendon Repair. J Hand Surg Am. 2016 Dec. 41 (12):e447-e452.
70. Calis M, Akgun K, Birtane M, et al: Diagnostic values of clinical diagnostic tests in subacromial impingement syndrome. Ann Rheum Dis 59(1):44–47, 2000.
71. Carson WC, Lovell WW, Whitesides TE: Congenital elevation of the scapula. J Bone Joint Surg Am 63:1199–1207, 1981.
72. Castagna A, Garofalo R, Cesari E, et al: Posterior superior internal impingement: an evidence-based review. Br J Sports Med 44:382–388, 2009.
73. Cavendish ME: Congenital elevation of the scapula. J Bone Joint Surg Br 54:395–408, 1972.
74. Chan K, MacDermid JC, Hoppe DJ, et al. Delayed versus early motion after arthroscopic rotator cuff repair: a meta-analysis. J Shoulder Elbow Surg. 2014 Aug 12.
75. Chang KV, Hung CY, Han DS, et al. Early Versus Delayed Passive Range of Motion Exercise for Arthroscopic Rotator Cuff Repair: A Meta-analysis of Randomized Controlled Trials. Am J Sports Med. 2014 Aug 20.
76. Chapter 5: Shoulder (Medscape)
77. Charousset C, Bellaiche L, Duranthon LD, et al: Accuracy of CT arthrography in the assessment of tears of the rotator cuff. J Bone Joint Surg Br 87:824–828, 2005.
78. Chiapat L, Palmer WE: Shoulder magnetic resonance imaging. Clin Sports Med 25:371–386, 2006.
79. Chronopoulus E, Kim TK, Park HB, et al: Diagnostic value of physical tests for isolated chronic acromioclavicular lesions. Am J Sports Med 32(3):655–661, 2004.
80. Clark HD, McCann PD: Acromioclavicular joint injuries. Orthop Clin North Am 31:177–187, 2000.
81. Clarkson HM: Musculoskeletal assessment: joint range of motion and manual muscle strength, ed 3, Philadelphia, 2013, Lippincott Williams & Wilkins.
82. Cleeman E, Flatow EL: Classification and diagnosis of impingement and rotator cuff lesions in athletes. Sports Med Arthro Rev 8:141–157, 2000.
83. Cleeman E, Flatow EL: Classification and diagnosis of impingement and rotator cuff lesions in athletes. Sports Med Arthro Rev 8:141–157, 2000.
84. Cofield RH, Irving JF: Evaluation and classification of shoulder instability. Clin Orthop 223:32–43, 1987.
85. Collaghan JJ, McNeish LM, Dehaven JP, et al: A prospective comparison study of double contrast computed tomography (CT) arthrography and arthroscopy of the shoulder. Am J Sports Med 16:13–20, 1988.
86. Collin PG, Gain S, Nguyen Huu F, Ladermann A. Is rehabilitation effective in massive rotator cuff tears?. Orthop Traumatol Surg Res. 2015 Jun. 101 (4 Suppl):S203-5.
87. Connell DA, Potter HG, Wickiewicz TL, et al: Noncontrast magnetic resonance imaging of superior labral lesions: 102 cases confirmed at arthroscopic surgery. Am J Sports Med 27:208–213, 1999.
88. Constant CR, Murley AHG: A clinical method of functional assessment of the shoulder. Clin Orthop 214:160–164, 1987.
89. Conte AL, Marques AP, Casarotto RA, Amado-João SM: Handedness influences passive shoulder range of motion in non athlete adult women. J Manip Physiol Ther 32:149–153, 2009.
90. Cook C, Beaty S, Kissenberth MJ, et al: Diagnostic accuracy of five orthopedic clinical tests for diagnosis of superior labrum anterior posterior (SLAP) lesions. J Shoulder Elbow Surg 21:13–22, 2012.
91. Cook C, Beaty S, Kissenberth MJ, et al: Diagnostic accuracy of five orthopedic clinical tests for diagnosis of superior labrum anterior posterior (SLAP) lesions. J Shoulder Elbow Surg 21:13–22, 2012.
92. Coppieters MW, Stappaerts KH, Everaert DG, et al: Addition of test components during neurodynamic testing: effect of range of motion and sensory responses. J Orthop Sports Phys Ther 31:226–237, 2001.
93. Cordasco FA, Bigliani LU: Large and massive tears: technique of open repair. Orthop Clin North Am 28:179–193, 1997.
94. Corrigan B, Maitland GD: Practical orthopedic medicine, London, 1985, Butterworths.
95. Corso G: Impingement relief test: an adjunctive procedure to traditional assessment of shoulder impingement syndrome. J Orthop Sports Phys Ther 22:183–192, 1995.
96. Cummins CA, Bowen M, Anderson K, et al: Suprascapular nerve entrapment at the spinoglenoid notch in a professional baseball pitcher. Am J Sports Med 27:810–812, 1999.
97. Cummins CA, Messer TM, Nuber GW: Suprascapular nerve entrapment. J Bone Joint Surg Am 82:415–424, 2000.
98. Curl LA, Warren RF: Glenohumeral joint stability: selective cutting studies on the static capsular restraints. Clin Orthop Relat Res 330:54–65, 1996.
99. Cusick MC, Cottrell BJ, Cain RA, et al: Low incidence of tendon rerupture after distal biceps repair by cortical button and interference screw. J Shoulder Elbow Surg. 2014 Oct. 23(10):1532-6.
100. Cyriax J: Textbook of orthopaedic medicine, vol 1: diagnosis of soft tissue lesions, London, 1982, Bailliere Tindall.
101. Davidson PA, Elattrache NS, Jobe CM, et al: Rotator cuff and posterosuperior glenoid labrum injury associated with increased glenohumeral motion: a new site of impingement. J Shoulder Elbow Surg 4:384–390, 1995.
102. Davidson PA, Elattrache NS, Jobe CM, et al: Rotator cuff and posterior-superior glenoid labrum injury associated with increased glenohumeral motion: a new site of impingement. J Shoulder Elbow Surg 4:384–390, 1995.
103. Davies GJ, Dickoff-Hoffman S: Neuromuscular testing and rehabilitation of the shoulder complex. J Orthop Sports Phys Ther 18:449–458, 1993.
104. Davies GJ, Gould JA, Larson RL: Functional examination of the shoulder girdle. Phys Sports Med 9:82–104, 1981.
105. Denaro V, Ruzzini L, Longo UG, et al. Effect of dihydrotestosterone on cultured human tenocytes from intact supraspinatus tendons. Knee Surg Sports Traumatol Arthrosc. 2010 Jul. 18(7):971-6.
106. Desmeules F, Minville L, Riederer B, et al: Acromiohumeral distance variation measured by ultrasonography and its association with the outcome of rehabilitation for shoulder impingement syndrome. Clin J Sport Med 14(4):197–205, 2004.
107. Dessaur WA, Magarey ME: Diagnostic accuracy of clinical tests

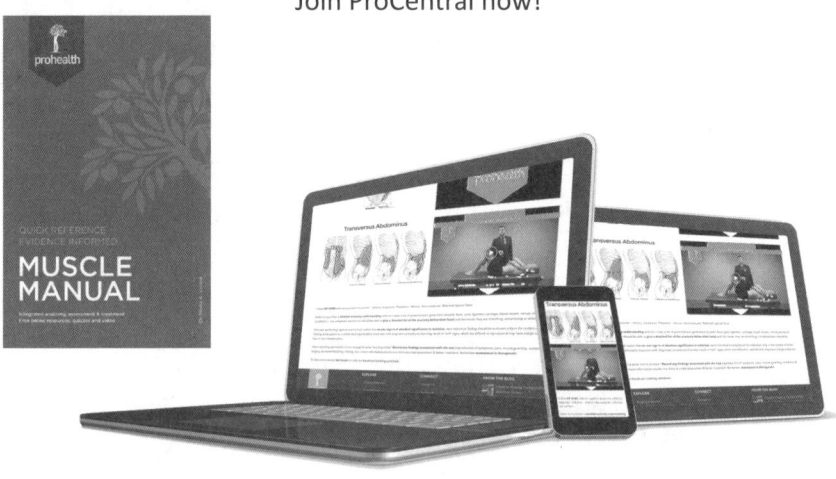

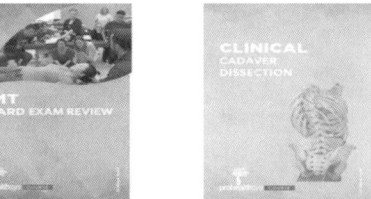

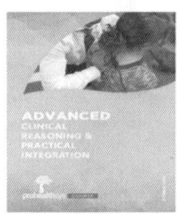

With low back pain people find it helpful / unhelpful when you ...

Helpful	Unhelpful
• Are confident and thorough	• Don't listen or interrupt to us
• Use humor (laughter)	• Give us scary information
• Take the time to listen	• Give us information we don't understand
• Can understand how pain has impacted my life (empathy)	• Don't write things down for us
• Put us in charge (with you as a coach)	• Don't support us
• Explain or pain (simple language)	• Don't involve us in our rehab plan
• Provide examples and resources	• Are in a hurry or rush us
• Reassure and build confidence	• Don't follow up
• Make us feel safe	• Overtreat us
• Help us become body aware	
• Provide clear instructions	
• Give us feedback	

Adapted from Holopainen R. Et al. Musculoskeletal care 2018.

Rectus Abdominus

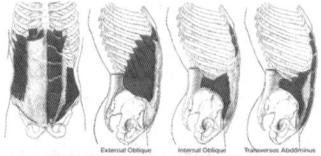

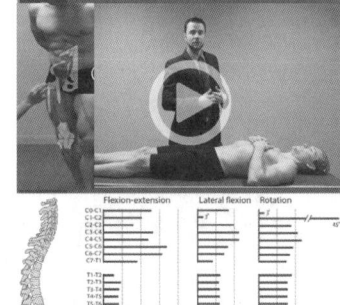

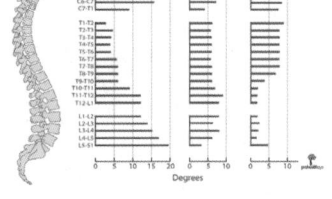

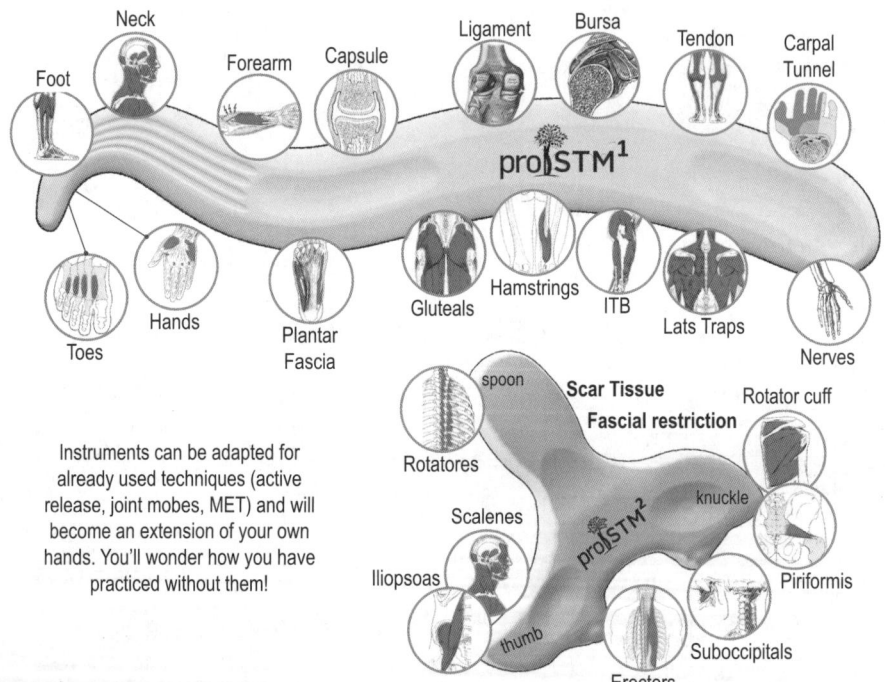

Instruments can be adapted for already used techniques (active release, joint mobes, MET) and will become an extension of your own hands. You'll wonder how you have practiced without them!

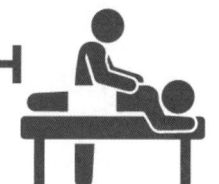

HOW TO CONNECT WITH YOUR PATIENTS!

PREPARE WITH INTENTION!
FAMILIARISE YOURSELF WITH THE PERSON BEFORE YOU MEET.

LISTEN INTENTLY + COMPLETELY!
SIT DOWN, LEAN TOWWARDS, DON'T INTERRUPT.

AGREE ON WHAT MATTERS MOST!
PRIORITISE WHAT YOUR PATIENT CARES ABOUT!

CONNECT WITH THEIR STORY!
ACKNOWLEDGE THEIR EFFORTS AND CONSIDER THEIR CIRCUMSTANCES.

EXPLORE THEIR EMOTIONAL CUES!
TUNE IN TO THEM, VALIDATE THEIR EMOTIONS TO BECOME A TRUSTED PARTNER.

DON'T LET "THE RESEARCH" GET IN THE WAY OF LOGIC AND CRITICAL THINKING

RESEARCH IS ONLY ONE PIECE OF THE PUZZLE, DON'T LET IT BLIND YOU

prohealthsys

Upgrade Your Practice
with ProCentral Education

success

WHAT PEOPLE SEE

WHAT PEOPLE DON'T SEE

prohealthsys

SACRIFICE

REJECTIONS

STAYING HEALTHY

SLEEPLESS NIGHTS

GOOD HABITS

DETERMINATION

GROWTH MINDSET

MEETING TARGETS

TEARS

FOCUS

PERSISTENCE

DISAPPOINTMENT

DAILY GOALS

TIME MANAGEMENT

LEARNING

DOUBTS

EXPENSES

RISK

TEAMWORK

ANXIETY

DISCIPLINE

You can do it. We can help!